SO-BBN-447

OCCASIONAL PAPER 134

India: Economic Reform and Growth

Ajai Chopra, Charles Collyns, Richard Hemming, and
Karen Parker with Woosik Chu and Oliver Fratzscher

FLORIDA STATE
UNIVERSITY LIBRARIES

OCT 1 7 2001

TALLAHASSEE, FLORIDA

INTERNATIONAL MONETARY FUND
Washington DC
December 1995

HC
435
.I757
1995

© 1995 International Monetary Fund

Cataloging-in-Publication Data

India: economic reform and growth/Ajai Chopra . . . [et al.]. —
   Washington, D.C. : International Monetary Fund, 1995
       p. cm. — (Occasional Paper, ISSN 0251-6365 ; 134)
    Includes bibliographical references.

   ISBN 1-55775-539-6

   1. India — Economic policy — 1980- . 2. Structural adjustment
(Economic policy) — India. 3. Investments — India. I. Chopra, Ajai.
II. Series: Occasional paper (International Monetary Fund) ; no. 134.
HC 435.2.I63   1995

Price: US$15.00
(US$12.00 to full-time faculty members and
students at universities and colleges)

Please send orders to:
International Monetary Fund, Publication Services
700 19th Street, N.W., Washington, D.C. 20431, U.S.A.
Tel.: (202) 623-7430   Telefax: (202) 623-7201
Internet: publications@imf.org

recycled paper

Contents

Charts

The following symbols have been used throughout this paper:

. . .   to indicate that data are not available;

—   to indicate that the figure is zero or less than half the final digit shown, or that the item does not exist;

–   between years or months (e.g., 1991–92 or January–June) to indicate the years or months covered, including the beginning and ending years or months;

/   between years (e.g., 1991/92) to indicate a crop or fiscal (financial) year.

"Billion" means a thousand million.

Minor discrepancies between constituent figures and totals are due to rounding.

The Indian financial year runs April 1–March 31.

The term "country," as used in this paper, does not in all cases refer to a territorial entity that is a state as understood by international law and practice; the term also covers some territorial entities that are not states, but for which statistical data are maintained and provided internationally on a separate and independent basis.

Preface

This report was prepared by a staff team in the Central Asia Department as background to the IMF's 1995 consultation (under Article IV) with India. It is one of a series of eight country case studies prepared as input for research into the relationship between adjustment and growth conducted in the Fiscal Affairs Department and the Policy Development and Review Department, which will be published in 1996. The authors acknowledge the valuable comments and ideas provided by Hubert Neiss, Bijan Aghevli, David Goldsbrough, and Anoop Singh. Melanie Dieckman provided excellent research assistance, while Nirmal Mohanty of the IMF's Delhi office helped assiduously to track down the data. Elena Frolia, Mila Villar, and Cathy Song provided unstinting secretarial support. The authors are also grateful to Esha Ray of the External Relations Department, who edited the paper for publication and coordinated production.

The views expressed here, as well as any errors, are the sole responsibility of the authors, and do not necessarily reflect the opinions of the Government of India, the Executive Directors of the IMF, or other members of the IMF staff.

The study was completed in June 1995, and is based on information available up to that time.

Abbreviations

BIFR	Board of Industrial and Financial Restructuring
CD	certificates of deposit
CRR	cash reserve requirement
FCCB	foreign currency convertible bond
FIPB	Foreign Investment Promotion Board
FII	foreign institutional investor
FRN	floating rate note
GDP	gross domestic product
GDR	global depository receipt
IIP	index of industrial production
LIBOR	London interbank offered rate
MODVAT	modified value-added tax
MoU	memorandum of understanding
NRF	National Renewal Fund
NRI	nonresident Indian
OECD	Organization for Economic Cooperation and Development
OPEC	Organization of Petroleum Exporting Countries
REER	real effective exchange rate
Sensex	Bombay Stock Exchange sensitivity index
SIA	Secretariat for Industrial Approvals
SLR	statutory liquidity ratio
TFP	total factor productivity
ULCRA	Urban Land Ceiling and Regulation Act
VAT	value-added tax
WPI	wholesale price index

I   Overview

Ajai Chopra and Charles Collyns

India has made substantial progress since 1991 on the path toward macroeconomic and structural reform. The benefits are becoming evident in a robust economic expansion, led by a recovery of private investment and rapid export growth. The external position has also strengthened considerably, while inflation has come down. Nonetheless, major economic policy challenges lie ahead, and the Indian Government will need to persevere with reform if India is to emulate the rapid economic growth and durable progress in poverty reduction achieved in countries in East Asia.

Long-Term Growth

Although India has generally followed prudent macroeconomic policies, its long-term growth record has been disappointing, with per capita income increasing by less than 2 percent annually since 1960. The fast-growing economies in East Asia, by contrast, recorded annual per capita growth rates of 5–6 percent during this period. Decades of pervasive government interference in economic decision making, together with an inward-oriented trade and investment policy, have resulted in low rates of return to investment in India and in excessively high capital-labor ratios.

Output and productivity growth showed a clearly improving trend during the 1980s. The shift was related primarily to changes in policies, including partial deregulation and increased market orientation. An additional element was a substantial real depreciation of the rupee, which provided a strong boost to exports. Furthermore, expansionary fiscal policies stimulated domestic demand, which played an important role in coaxing extra output from the economy, although growth of this nature could not be sustained.

Response to the 1991 Crisis

Since 1991, the Indian authorities have made a determined effort to correct many of the serious distortions in the economy and to reduce pervasive state intervention. The initial impetus came from a severe balance of payments crisis in 1990–91. That crisis prompted the Indian authorities to adopt an adjustment program that contained both immediate stabilization measures and ambitious structural reforms. Despite some policy slippage, the stabilization effort proved sufficient to restore external confidence and led to the buildup of foreign exchange reserves. After an initial period of slow growth, the economy responded vigorously to the reforms.

In the early stages of the adjustment program, India placed considerable emphasis on reducing imports temporarily through administrative controls. Subsequently, stabilization measures centered on monetary tightening and fiscal consolidation, supported by a devaluation. Structural reforms were initially concentrated in the industrial sector and in trade liberalization—aimed particularly at eliminating most investment and import licensing requirements. The foreign investment regime was also liberalized substantially. The focus then shifted to tax reform, further trade liberalization (including continued reductions in tariffs), and financial sector reform.

Results of Adjustment

The fiscal retrenchment and monetary tightening in response to the crisis led to a contraction of demand. This, combined with the withdrawal of external financing and restrictions on imports, contributed to a slowdown in economic growth to 1 percent in fiscal year 1991/92 (April 1–March 31). The downturn was short-lived, however, as the external financing constraint eased considerably after 1991. Indeed, beginning in 1993, private capital inflows surged. The surge, combined with the demand stimulus arising from a widening of the fiscal deficit in 1993/94, buoyant export growth, and a growing investment response to the reform program, helped generate a broadly based economic recovery. Growth rebounded to $4^{1}/_{2}$ percent annually in both 1992/93 and 1993/94 and reached $6^{1}/_{4}$ percent in

Table 1.1. Key Economic Indicators

	1990/91	1991/92	1992/93	1993/94	Est. 1994/95
	(Percent change)				
Real GDP growth	5.4	0.9	4.3	4.3	6.2
Wholesale prices (end-period)	12.1	13.6	7.0	10.8	10.4
Export volume	3.7	–2.0	3.8	23.4	14.2
Import volume	6.5	–20.2	8.8	8.7	21.4
	(In percent of GDP)				
Central government deficit	8.6	6.3	5.7	7.7	6.7
Consolidated public sector deficit	10.5	9.0	8.4	11.0	10.5
External current account deficit	3.4	0.7	1.6	0.3	0.5
	(In billions of U.S. dollars)				
Gross official reserves					
End-period	2.2	5.6	6.4	15.1	20.8
In months of imports	1.0	3.2	3.3	7.6	8.5

Sources: Data provided by the Indian authorities; and IMF staff estimates.

1994/95, three years after the launching of reforms (Table 1.1).

The performance of various sectors has nonetheless diverged substantially. Initially, industrial growth fell well below its long-term trend, while growth in agriculture and services was steadier. Signs of an industrial recovery emerged beginning in the first quarter of 1992/93, but the recovery stalled toward the end of the year and did not resume until late 1993/94. In the following period, industrial growth picked up markedly. In particular, the capital goods sector, which had suffered a sharp recession for three years and had previously been heavily protected, bounced back vigorously with production rising by about 20 percent in 1994/95.

Real gross fixed investment declined sharply in 1991/92 and recovered slowly in the following two years. The downturn resulted mainly from tight financial policies, which raised the cost of credit to the private sector. The available evidence points to a resurgence of private investment in 1994/95. This would be consistent with the recovery of industrial production, increased credit availability, rising corporate profitability, and growing business confidence.

Fiscal Initiatives

Stabilization of the Indian economy owed much to the initial fiscal adjustment undertaken by the central government, which increased the credibility of macroeconomic policy. Given the subsequent fiscal slippage at the center, however, and a deterioration

of the states' fiscal position, the consolidated public sector deficit in 1994/95 remained close to the deficit in 1990/91. The continuing large deficit and high public indebtedness raise concerns about the sustainability of fiscal policy. Increasing pressures on real interest rates have emerged, and these threaten to crowd out private investment. These fiscal pressures underscore the need to strengthen state finances, given the risk that fiscal adjustment by the central government could be undermined by expansionary policies by states.

Turning to the structure of government finances, substantial progress has been made toward creating a simpler and fairer tax system. A principal feature of the tax reform has been the general lowering of tax rates. This, together with a narrowing of the dispersion in tax rates, has helped reduce distortions and disincentives. Nevertheless, additional efforts by both the central government and state governments are needed to broaden the tax base and reduce distortions further. Less has been achieved on the expenditure side. The interest burden is substantial, with the composition of noninterest spending skewed toward unproductive expenditures. Furthermore, inadequate attention to infrastructure and education—both primarily state responsibilities—have large spillover costs.

Structural Reforms

In the last four years, India has introduced major reforms to improve the efficiency of resource allocation and expand the productive capacity of the economy. The reforms have focused on liberalizing product markets, particularly by removing impediments to domestic and foreign private investment and liberalizing the trade and external payments regime. The liberalization of factor markets has so far centered on financial markets, with emphasis on increasing the role of market mechanisms in credit allocation.

The private sector's response to these reforms has been impressive:

- Trade liberalization has led to an increasingly open economy; the ratio of exports and imports of goods and nonfactor services to GDP rose to more than 23 percent in 1994/95 from an average of 15 percent in the 1980s.
- Investment picked up markedly in 1994/95, notably in such areas as automobiles and consumer electronics. New private enterprises have been established in banking and other financial services, commercial aviation, and software development, while major investments are taking place in telecommunications, power, petrochemicals, and oil exploration.
- The reforms have stimulated the interest of foreign investors, with foreign investment surging in the year beginning in November 1993. During this period, India accounted for a larger volume of international equity issues than any other emerging market. Shares purchased on local exchanges were also heavy, while foreign direct investment increased substantially.

The Road Ahead

Although much has been accomplished, the reforms are by no means complete, and persisting obstacles constrain a stronger and broader investment response. The overall fiscal deficit needs to be reduced substantially to relieve pressure on domestic savings. And despite efforts to attract private investment, inadequate infrastructure remains a major barrier. Moreover, little has been done to address the serious distortions in public enterprises, labor markets, and the agricultural sector. Further reforms in these areas, implemented in a steady and transparent fashion, are essential for sustaining rapid growth in

India. Indeed, broadening the reforms to cover agriculture—which employs the bulk of the population—should spread the benefits of reform and help improve income distribution.

The following policy areas also merit attention:

- Tariff rates remain relatively high by international standards, while imports of consumer goods and trade in agricultural commodities continue to be subject to quantitative restrictions.
- A number of important internal restrictions remain on private sector activity (for example, reserving certain sectors of the economy for small-scale enterprises), which constrain the development of key sectors of the economy. Reforms have also lagged at the state level, where distortions and inefficiencies remain widespread.
- Limited progress in restructuring public enterprises and in reforming inflexible labor and property laws has perpetuated the inefficient use of a sizable part of India's capital and labor force.
- Limited progress in fiscal consolidation has hampered financial sector reform. Although the cash reserve requirement and the statutory liquidity ratio have been lowered, the flow of funds from the banking system to the public sector remains substantial.

The sections that follow analyze India's growth record and the impact of macroeconomic and structural policies implemented since 1991 on investment and growth. Section II reviews longer-term trends for growth and factor accumulation, based in part on a "growth accounting" framework. Section III documents the response of the economy since the launching of the reform and stabilization program in 1991. Section IV examines in more detail the behavior of private investment, particularly the impact of financial policies. The implications of fiscal adjustment and reform for growth are analyzed in Section V. Section VI reviews the recent experience with a surge in capital inflows and assesses its impact on the Indian economy. Finally, Section VII investigates the impact of recent structural reforms on investment and growth and identifies a number of remaining structural impediments.

II   Long-Term Growth Trends

Ajai Chopra

For most of the period since independence, India has combined a highly interventionist and inward-looking approach to economic development with generally conservative macroeconomic policies. The development strategy was to build a large, publicly owned, heavy industry sector while leaving the production of consumer goods (imports of which were banned) and agriculture mainly to the private sector. To support this strategy, India relied on a complex system of industrial licensing, high protection against imports, and extensive government intervention in financial intermediation. Macroeconomic policies were driven by the overriding desire for stability and low inflation; on the whole, public sector deficits were moderate and monetary growth was low. Household savings grew quite rapidly as the deleterious effects of financial repression were partly mitigated by low inflation, the spread of bank branches, and the introduction of small savings schemes.

Output, Investment, and Macroeconomic Conditions

Economic performance since independence has been mixed. Once the initial impetus of large investment for import substitution subsided, low productivity increases in inefficient public enterprises together with weather-related fluctuations in agricultural output constrained the growth of economic activity. Overall growth slowed from an average of some 3½ percent a year in the 1950s and the 1960s to about 2½ percent a year in the 1970s (see Chart 2.1 and Table 2.1). Manufacturing and services have grown relatively more rapidly, resulting in a decline

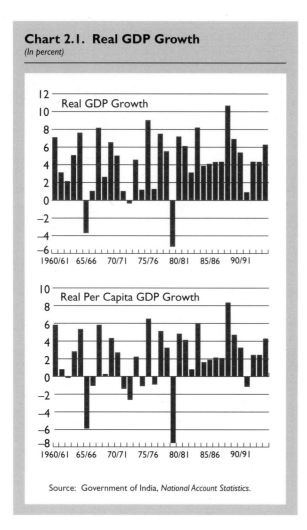

Chart 2.1. Real GDP Growth
(In percent)

Source: Government of India, *National Account Statistics.*

Table 2.1. Compound Annual Rates of Growth
(In percent)

	1960/61– 1994/95	1960/61– 1969/70	1970/71– 1979/80	1980/81– 1989/90	1990/91– 1994/95
Real GDP	4.1	3.6	2.6	5.7	4.1
Real per capita GDP	1.8	1.3	0.3	3.5	1.2

Source: Government of India, *National Account Statistics.*

Chart 2.2 Structure of GDP
(In percent)

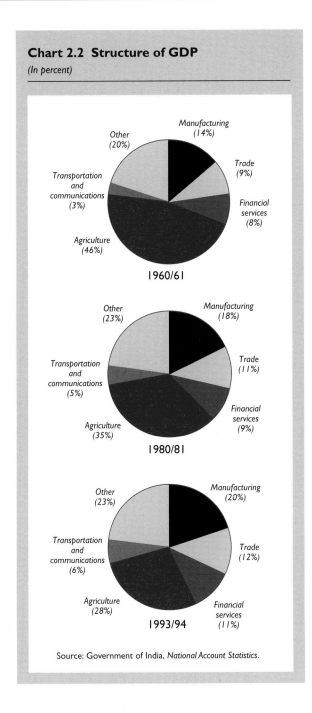

Source: Government of India, *National Account Statistics.*

Table 2.2. Average Investment and Domestic Savings[1]
(In percent of GDP)

	1960/61–1993/94	1960/61–1969/70	1970/71–1979/80	1980/81–1989/90	1990/91–1993/94
Investment	19.4	15.6	19.1	22.0	23.3
Private	10.7	8.5	10.7	11.6	14.1
Public	8.7	7.1	8.4	10.4	9.2
Savings	18.0	13.5	18.9	20.0	21.7
Private	15.0	10.7	15.2	17.0	20.5
Public	2.9	2.7	3.7	3.0	1.2

Source: Ministry of Finance (1995).
[1]Investment figures are for gross domestic capital formation, with errors and omissions allocated to the private sector. Savings figures are for gross domestic savings.

gross domestic capital formation increased by a compound rate of 4.4 percent a year between 1960/61 and 1993/94, compared with 4 percent for GDP. Domestic savings, particularly of the private sector, were high and rose broadly in line with investment (Table 2.2). Both investment and domestic savings in India, however, remain substantially below those of fast-growing East Asian economies such as Indonesia, Malaysia, Singapore, and Thailand (Chart 2.3).

In the absence of large imbalances between investment and domestic savings, the external accounts were generally satisfactory. Current account deficits were financed by large aid inflows, while official reserves were maintained at a comfortable level (Chart 2.4). With a cautious monetary policy, inflation reached double-digit levels only sporadically in the wake of unfavorable harvests or external shocks (Chart 2.5).

A number of important changes took place in the 1980s that set the stage for an increase in growth, but also a rise in inflation and a deterioration in the external accounts. First, dissatisfaction with the prolonged period of slow growth prompted the first steps in a process of gradual liberalization. Industrial licensing requirements were eased, exporters were given greater access to imports, some quantitative restrictions were replaced by tariffs, and toward the end of the decade there was a modest liberalization of financial markets. Second, the exchange rate depreciated by 45 percent in real effective terms during the 1980s (Chart 2.5), which provided a strong stimulus to previously lackluster export growth. Third, the deficit of the central government widened, rising to about 8–9 percent of

in the share of agriculture in GDP (Chart 2.2). The share of GDP produced by the public sector, however, increased steadily from 10 percent in the early 1960s to 18 percent in 1980/81 and further to nearly 27 percent in 1990/91.

Underlying these growth trends was an increase in the rate of both public and private investment, with the total rising from about 15 percent of GDP in the early 1960s to 25 percent by the late 1980s. Investment has grown somewhat faster than output as

Chart 2.3 Saving and Investment in Selected Countries[1]

(In percent of GDP)

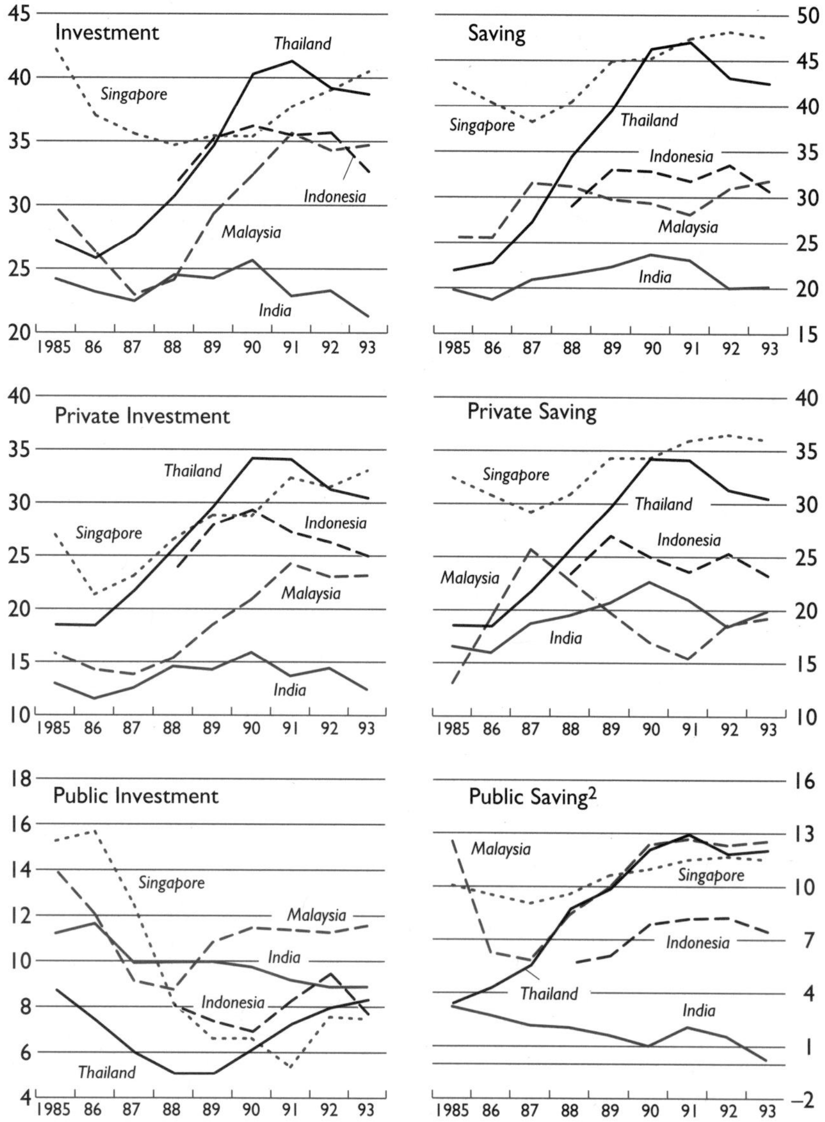

Source: IMF staff estimates.

[1]Fiscal year for India (that is, 1985 = 1985/86).

[2]Refers to general government saving.

GDP from the mid-1980s onward (Chart 2.6). The fiscal deterioration mainly resulted from rising current expenditures, especially for interest and subsidies, with loans and grants to states, wages, and defense also contributing. Thus, the fiscal impulse during the 1980s averaged 0.5 percent of GDP a year, compared with 0.1 percent of GDP a year in the previous two decades.[1]

---

[1]The fiscal impulse measure used here is the same as that used in the IMF's World Economic Outlook exercise. It is calculated by separating the actual budget balance into two components: a

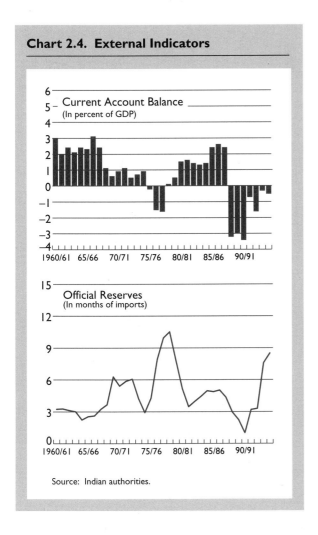

Chart 2.4. External Indicators

Source: Indian authorities.

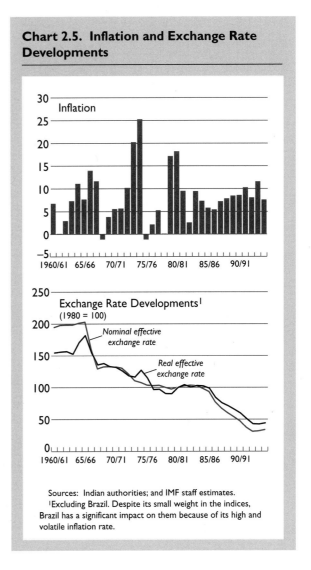

Chart 2.5. Inflation and Exchange Rate Developments

Sources: Indian authorities; and IMF staff estimates.
[1]Excluding Brazil. Despite its small weight in the indices, Brazil has a significant impact on them because of its high and volatile inflation rate.

The combination of strong domestic demand, rapid export growth, and more liberal supply-side policies supported a broad-based increase in average output growth to over 5½ percent a year during the 1980s. However, with the large government deficit fueling rapid credit expansion and with the continuing depreciation of the rupee, inflation rose from about 5 percent in the mid-1980s to over 12 percent at the end of 1990/91. Moreover, notwithstanding the unprecedented growth of exports, the current ac-

count deficit widened from under 2 percent of GDP during the early part of the decade to 3.5 percent of GDP in 1990/91. These deficits were increasingly financed by borrowing on commercial terms, including inflows of short-term deposits by nonresident Indians, while official reserves were drawn down. These developments led to a marked rise in the external debt-service burden (Table 2.3).

Education, Labor, Employment, and Poverty

Steady growth has led to gradual improvements in social indicators such as life expectancy, infant mortality, and literacy. Similarly, the incidence of poverty has declined, although it remains a serious problem.

cyclically neutral component and a fiscal stance component. The cyclically neutral component is defined by assuming that government expenditures increase proportionately to nominal trend output and that government revenues increase proportionately to nominal actual output. The fiscal stance component—the residual between the cyclically neutral and the actual budget balance—then captures the full effect of automatic stabilizers and discretionary changes in fiscal policy. The fiscal impulse is the annual change in the fiscal stance measure, expressed as a share of GDP. A negative number would indicate a contractionary demand impulse emanating from fiscal policy, and a positive number would indicate an expansionary demand impulse.

Chart 2.6 Public Sector Accounts
(In percent of GDP)

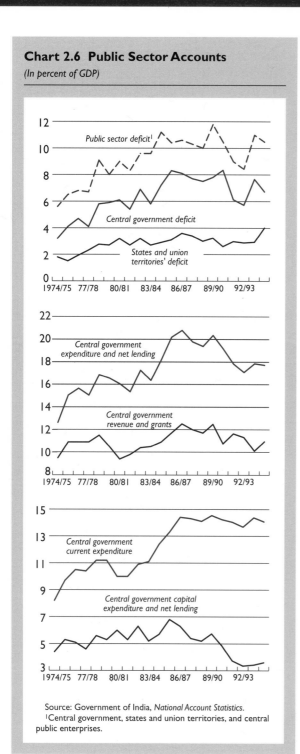

Source: Government of India, *National Account Statistics*.
[1]Central government, states and union territories, and central public enterprises.

Moreover, data on the stock of educational attainment compiled by Barro and Lee (1993) show that much of the improvement between 1960 and 1985 was due to increased secondary education, while the proportion of the population completing primary school actually declined (Table 2.5). Still, in 1985, 70 percent of the population had received no formal schooling. These observations are at variance with the well-accepted notion that the returns for primary education are higher than the returns for secondary and higher levels of education.[2]

The annual growth rate of the labor force fell from about 2.5 percent during the 1970s and early 1980s to 1.4 percent between 1983 and 1987/88.[3] A fall in the labor participation rate led to the decline, as a larger number of children and young persons withdrew from the labor force to attend school.[4]

The great majority of the labor force is employed in the informal sector. Employment in the formal or organized sector of the economy has been constrained by rigidities arising from legislation that only applies to this part of the market. The proportion of employment in the organized sector has remained essentially unchanged at 8 percent of total employment. Growth in organized sector employment has been dominated by the public sector, while private employment in this sector has been stagnant (Table 2.6).[5]

According to the International Labor Organization (1993), overall employment improved in the 1980s as both rural and urban underemployment fell substantially. The rise in the real wage rate for casual labor in both sectors provides further evidence of some tightening of labor markets. Rural employment improved largely because of the rapid growth of nonagricultural employment. Employment in the organized segment of the urban economy, however, grew at a much slower rate than it had done in the 1970s, despite the rapid growth of output in this sector.

With underemployment being the immediate source of poverty, the pace of poverty reduction also increased in the 1980s (Table 2.7).[6] Poverty remains overwhelmingly a rural phenomenon. Nevertheless, along with the urbanization of the population, urban poverty has also risen.

---

[2]See, for example, Psacharopoulos (1993).
[3]See International Labor Organization (1993).
[4]A moderate decline in the rate of population increase also contributed to the slowing of labor force growth.
[5]The organized sector includes all establishments in the public sector irrespective of the number of employees and nonagricultural establishments in the private sector employing ten or more persons.
[6]The International Labor Organization (1993) report notes that the poor live in households that have few assets other than labor resources and poverty arises fundamentally because these labor resources cannot find adequate and adequately remunerative employment.

Indicators of educational attainment have also improved steadily over the past three decades; gross enrollment ratios have risen and illiteracy rates have fallen. Nevertheless, these indicators still lag far behind those of most East Asian countries (Table 2.4).

Table 2.3. Debt Indicators
(In percent)

	1979/80	1984/85	1989/90	1994/95
Central government debt				
Domestic/GDP	40.4	45.7	54.6	54.1
External/GDP	8.7	9.3	12.2	5.6
Total debt/GDP	49.1	55.0	66.8	59.7
External debt				
Debt/GDP	12.6	17.1	27.7	31.6
Debt/exports	142.0	251.9	358.2	269.3
Debt service/exports	10.2	22.6	31.5	31.8
Interest/exports	3.7	13.4	17.4	11.6

Sources: Joshi and Little (1994), Table 9.2; and IMF staff estimates.

Growth, Accumulation, and Productivity

The longer-term trends described above indicate that India has generated reasonably high rates of both investment and savings and that the macroeconomic situation has generally been stable.[7] Yet, India's growth record has been disappointing relative to the fast-growing economies in East Asia. By implication, productivity in India has risen only modestly. Empirical studies, in which the rate of growth is related to the rate of accumulation of productive assets and total factor productivity (TFP), support this proposition.[8]

One approach to examining relative contributions of factor accumulation and productivity growth assumes that production technology is characterized by constant returns to scale. TFP growth is then calculated by subtracting from output growth the contributions made by labor and capital accumulation.

---

[7]The empirical results reported in this section are from Goldsbrough and others (forthcoming).

[8]These models generally decompose growth into the contributions of factors such as capital (physical and human) and labor. Typically, however, output growth cannot be explained fully by increases in these factors. The part of growth not explained by the factors of production—that is, the residual—usually reflects more efficient use of resources or the adoption of new production technologies; in other words, improvements in total factor productivity.

Table 2.4. India and Selected Country Groupings: Indicators of Educational Attainment

	20–25 Years Ago India	10–15 Years Ago India	Most Recent Estimates		
			India	South Asia[1]	East Asia[1]
Gross enrollment ratio					
Primary school[2]	79	96	106	106	130
Secondary school	26	38	44	40	50
Number of students per teacher					
Primary school	42	58	63	61	23
Secondary school	21	21	26	26	16
Illiteracy rate (percent of population over 7)[3]	66	56	48	54	24

Sources: World Bank, *Social Indicators of Development;* and Ministry of Finance (1995).

[1]Consistent with the definitions of the World Bank's *World Development Report,* South Asia covers the Islamic State of Afghanistan, Bangladesh, Bhutan, India, Nepal, Pakistan, and Sri Lanka; and East Asia covers Cambodia, China, Indonesia, the Democratic People's Republic of Korea, the Republic of Korea, the Lao People's Democratic Republic, Malaysia, Mongolia, Myanmar, Papua New Guinea, the Philippines, Thailand, and Vietnam.

[2]Gross enrollment may be reported in excess of 100 percent if some pupils are younger or older than the country's standard range of primary school age (typically 6–11 years for primary school).

[3]For South Asia and East Asia comparators, illiteracy rates are for percent of population over 15 years of age.

Table 2.5. Stock of Educational Attainment
(Percent of population over age of 25 years)

	1960	1985
Completed primary school	6.3	4.5
Completed secondary school	0.9	5.4
No schooling	75.5	69.8
Average number of years in school[1]	1.4	3.1

Source: Barro and Lee (1993).

[1]Although the average number of years of schooling in India has risen considerably, it remains well below that of East Asian and Pacific economies, where it increased from 2.3 years in 1960 to 5.2 years in 1985.

Table 2.6. Employment in the Organized Sector

	1978	1983	1988	1993
Total				
In millions	21.2	24.0	25.7	27.2
As percent of total employment	8.0	7.9	8.0	...
Share (in percent) of				
Public sector	67.0	68.8	71.2	71.2
Private sector	33.0	31.2	28.8	28.8

Sources: Ministry of Finance (1995); and International Labor Organization (1993).

Table 2.7. Rural and Urban Population Below the Poverty Line
(In percent of rural or urban population)

	1970/71	1977/78	1983	1988/89
Rural	57	55	50	43
Urban	45	43	38	35
Memorandum items:				
Percentage of total poor in				
Rural areas	84	82	80	78
Urban areas	16	18	20	22

Source: International Labor Organization (1993).

Table 2.8. India and Selected Country Groupings: Factor Contributions to Output Growth[1]
(Average annual percent change in real terms)

	GDP	Capital	Labor	Total Factor Productivity (Solow Residuals)
(Period: 1960–88)				
East Asia[2]	7.4	3.8	1.7	1.9
South Asia[3]	3.6	1.8	1.2	0.6
Of which:				
India	3.1	1.7	1.0	0.3
Africa	3.4	1.8	1.3	0.3
Latin America	3.8	1.8	1.5	0.4
OECD	3.7	1.8	0.7	1.2
(Period: 1980–88)				
East Asia[2]	6.2	3.2	1.4	1.6
South Asia[3]	4.5	1.8	1.4	1.3
Of which:				
India	4.8	1.3	1.2	2.3
Africa	2.1	1.2	1.4	−0.5
Latin America	1.2	0.9	1.6	−1.4
OECD	2.4	1.0	0.8	0.6

Sources: IMF staff estimates based on Fischer (1993) formulation and data, with the exception of capital growth data, which are taken from King and Levine (1994). Summers and Heston (1994) data for real GDP growth in constant international prices and World Bank data for labor force growth were used.

[1]The contributions of capital and labor are derived by multiplying their respective growth rates by the share of each factor in output. Factor shares are imposed as 0.4 for capital and 0.6 for labor. Total factor productivity (the Solow residual) is calculated as the residual after taking account of the contributions of capital and labor.

[2]Includes only high-performing East Asian economies: Hong Kong, Indonesia, the Republic of Korea, Malaysia, Singapore, Taiwan Province of China, and Thailand.

[3]Includes Bangladesh, India, Nepal, Pakistan, and Sri Lanka.

The results of this exercise for India, as well as for other country groups, are presented in Table 2.8.[9] These results show that the high-performing East Asian countries grew significantly faster than India because of much faster growth of their capital stocks as well as higher TFP growth. The results for the subperiod 1980–88 suggest, however, that India's productivity improved markedly in the 1980s to lev-

---

[9]The TFP estimates in Table 2.8 are referred to as the "Solow residuals" and assume a production function in which factor shares are 0.4 for capital and 0.6 for labor. TFP estimates assuming a function that also includes human capital as a factor of production, as in Mankiw, Romer, and Weil (1992), were also calculated. The two sets of TFP estimates were highly correlated.

Chart 2.7. Contribution of Total Factor Productivity to Growth[1]

(In percent)

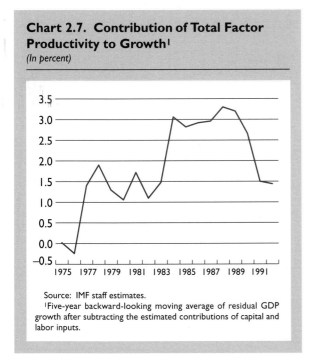

Source: IMF staff estimates.

[1]Five-year backward-looking moving average of residual GDP growth after subtracting the estimated contributions of capital and labor inputs.

gression (see Table 2.9), India's rate of factor accumulation and its relatively low starting position could have been expected to result in per capita income growth of about 1.9 percent a year between 1960 and 1992; actual growth over this period was 2.2 percent, suggesting that about 15 percent of long-term growth in India is attributable to influences other than the accumulation of factors of production. By contrast, for a group of successful East Asian countries, an average of some 40 percent of long-term growth is attributable to other influences. Compared with world "average" growth, however, India's growth performance has been reasonably good.

The link between macroeconomic and structural conditions and growth is examined next. Following Fischer (1993), time series and cross-country regression analysis can be used to examine correlations between the various proxy measures for the impact of policies, and output growth, factor accumulation, and TFP growth. The evidence suggests that macroeconomic instability is associated with lower growth and that the links operate through a dampening of both investment and productivity.[10] Specifically, high inflation, budget

els comparable to East Asia, contributing to the acceleration in output growth in the 1980s (Chart 2.7).

Another approach to analyzing growth performance relies on cross-country regressions that relate per capita income growth to investment in human and physical capital, while controlling for the population growth rate and initial level of per capita income. Based on the parameters from such a re-

[10]In view of the difficulty in constructing measures of variables that are directly controlled by policies, it becomes necessary to proxy policies and distortions using variables that can be both the outcome of policies and also affected by nonpolicy-related factors. Thus, the policy implications of the observed linkages between these proxy variables and growth should be drawn with caution. Moreover, the estimated equations should not be viewed as structural equations explaining growth.

Table 2.9. Contribution of Accumulation to Growth[1]

Variable	Parameter Estimate	Sample Mean	Contribution to Growth (In percent)
Intercept	−0.07	1.0	−0.07
Relative GDP to the United States, 1960	−3.77	0.1	−0.29
Primary enrollment, 1960	1.23	0.6	0.75
Secondary enrollment, 1960	0.74	0.2	0.15
Growth of population	−0.19	2.2	−0.42
Investment/GDP	0.13	13.8	1.77
Adjusted R-square	0.45		
Actual growth			2.22
Predicted growth			1.88
Percent of actual growth predicted			85

Sources: IMF staff estimates. Data for per capita growth, investment, GDP relative to the United States, and population are taken from Summers and Heston (1994). Primary and secondary school enrollment data are taken from the World Bank's World Tables.

[1]The dependent variable for the regression was per capita income growth, measured at international prices. The regression was estimated for 103 countries over the 1960–92 period.

Table 2.10. Impact of Policies on Growth, Capital Accumulation, and Factor Productivity, 1970–92

(In percent)

	Estimated Correlation with Growth[1]	Estimated Correlation with Capital Accumulation[1]	Estimated Correlation with TFP Growth[1]	India	Whole Sample	Asian Developing Countries	East Asia	OECD
Macroeconomic policies								
Inflation	—	—	—	8.7	22.0[2]	9.9	8.1	9.3
Budget surplus[3]	+	—	++	−6.3	−4.3	−3.3	−1.6	−4.1
Capital expenditures[3]	+++	+++	...	1.9	4.7	4.8	5.3	2.8
Government savings[3]	+++	+++	++	−4.4	0.5	1.4	3.7	−1.2
Exchange rate premium	—	—	...	20.2	75.4	48.7	4.0	0.8
External conditions								
Change in the terms of trade	+++	...	+++	−0.9	−0.4	−0.1	0.9	−0.2
Structural policies								
Primary school enrollment rate	+++	...	++	72.0	85.1	82.8	95.7	106.0
Ratio of broad money to GDP	...	++	...	36.1	39.0	37.4	46.7	61.4
Average effective import tax rate	...	—	...	24.9	13.4	14.7	12.1	11.6
GDP in 1970 (in logarithms)	—	—	...	2.9	3.3	3.1	3.3	3.9
Memorandum items:								
Real GDP growth				4.3	3.4	5.6	7.4	2.7
Growth in real capital stock				4.4	4.2	6.7	9.9	3.6
Growth in total factor productivity (TFP)				1.4	0.3	1.4	1.8	0.4

Source: IMF staff estimates.

[1]The correlations are estimated from three panel regressions with growth in real GDP, capital accumulation, and TFP as dependent variables. TFP residuals are calculated as follows: TFP = ZGDP − 0.4 ZKAP − 0.6 ZLAB, where ZGDP is the rate of growth of real GDP, ZKAP is the rate of growth in the real capital stock, and ZLAB is the growth rate of the labor force. The data for ZGDP and GDP in 1970 are measured at purchasing power parity prices and are taken from Summers and Heston (1994); data for ZKAP are from King and Levine (1994); data for the budget surplus, government capital expenditure and savings, and the average effective import tax rate are from the IMF's *Government Finance Statistics Yearbook*; data for inflation and broad money are from the IMF's *International Financial Statistics*; and all other variables are from Fischer (1993). The symbols +++ and ⸺ mean that the correlations are significant at the 1 percent level, and ++(⸺) and +(−) imply significance at the 5 and 10 percent levels, respectively.

[2]Whole sample averages for inflation exclude Argentina, Bolivia, Brazil, and Nicaragua.

[3]In percent of GDP. The effects of the budget deficit, on the one hand, and capital expenditures and government savings, on the other, were estimated in separate panel regressions. The estimated effects of the other macroeconomic variables did not differ significantly between the two regressions.

deficits, and parallel exchange market premiums are all associated with lower output growth. The results also suggest that structural distortions—proxied, for example, by high tariff protection and an underdeveloped financial system—and low educational attainment are negatively correlated with output and capital accumulation.

Table 2.10 presents the estimated correlations of macroeconomic and structural factors with the growth of output, capital, and TFP growth and compares the sample averages for the "policy" variables in India with those of other country groupings. Compared with the whole sample, India's macroeconomic policies—with one important exception—were conducive to relatively rapid output growth, capital accumulation, and productivity gains. The exception is fiscal policy, which has likely had a negative influence on long-term growth, as India's performance regarding the budget deficit, government capital expenditures, and government savings was noticeably worse than for other country groupings. In addition, the measure of tariff protection in India is quite high by international standards, suggesting that distortions in the trade regime are likely to have been an important factor explaining India's poor growth performance relative to other Asian countries.[11] The measure of human capital accumulation is also low by international standards, suggesting that insufficient investment in education could

[11]Moreover, with significant quantitative restrictions, especially for consumer goods imports, in place for the period under study, the indicator of protection is biased downward in the case of India.

Table 2.11. Productivity Trends in Manufacturing by End-Use
(Percent change a year, compound)

	Total Factor Productivity		Labor Productivity		Capital Productivity	
	1960–80	1981–89	1960–80	1981–89	1960–80	1981–89
Manufacturing	–0.5	2.7	2.1	7.3	–2.8	–0.7
Intermediate	–1.4	2.4	1.8	7.1	–4.0	–0.3
Capital goods	1.5	2.0	4.4	5.7	–1.6	–0.9
Consumer durables	1.0	2.6	3.5	7.6	–2.2	–1.2
Consumer nondurables	–0.5	3.8	1.4	8.8	–2.1	–0.1

Source: Ahluwalia (1995).

have impeded more rapid capital accumulation and long-term growth. The financial development indicator, however, suggests that India's financial market is relatively well developed by international standards.

Results of India-Specific Studies

The most comprehensive study of TFP trends in India is that of Ahluwalia (1991).[12] Her study examined the growth of TFP in the organized manufacturing sector (which accounts for 11.5 percent of GDP) from 1960 to 1989. Using data on value added, capital stocks, employment, and wages collected from the Annual Survey of Industries, she estimated annual TFP by industry as the difference between value added and weighted shares of capital and labor inputs. The results, which are summarized in Table 2.11, indicate that after a long period of stagnation during 1960–80, TFP growth improved significantly in the 1980s.[13] The overall improvement reflects improvements in both labor and capital productivity.

To account for variations in TFP growth across industries, Ahluwalia ran cross-industry regressions of TFP as a function of various factors. Several significant conclusions emerge. Industries established for import substitution (for example, capital goods) experienced lower TFP growth. By encouraging industries lacking a market-based reason for growth, inef-

ficient enterprises were promoted. Moreover, industries with high capital-to-labor ratios at the beginning of the period of study had lower rates of TFP growth. A possible explanation is that those industries with high capital-to-labor ratios were the ones targeted by the government as part of its heavy industry promotion. Under the relatively stringent control of government regulation, these industries tended to show lower rates of TFP growth. Indeed, Ahluwalia (1995) notes that a significant feature of the Indian industrial experience has been a sharply rising capital-labor ratio over the period 1960–90. This trend reflects both the inflexibility of labor laws with respect to hiring and firing, thus making labor much more costly than suggested by the real wage rate, and the bias toward capital intensity, which is inherent in a highly protective trade policy regime.

Joshi and Little (1994) estimated real rates of return to investment in India in the public sector and in organized manufacturing of the private sector from 1960/61 through 1986/87.[14] They focused on two distinct time periods—1960/61 to 1975/76 and 1976/77 to 1986/87—to assess whether a discernable change in the returns to investment had taken place. They found that the rates of return on public investment, especially in manufacturing, were very low in both periods (Table 2.12), which they attribute in part to the allocation procedures for public investment (for example, inadequate project appraisal and political factors) that resulted in investment in sectors where India had little comparative advantage. In contrast, rates of return on private manufacturing nearly doubled from the first period to the next, to a level comparable to those found in industrial countries.

---

[12]An update of this study is contained in Ahluwalia (1995).

[13]In an attempt to improve on the Ahluwalia study, Balakrishnan and Pushpangadan (1994) use a double-deflation method to construct a time series of value added. Using this time series, they do not find that TFP growth improved in the 1980s. Ahluwalia (1995), however, questions these new results because of the empirical compromises made in the process of attempting to derive the price index for intermediate inputs to perform the double deflation.

---

[14]Estimates for the whole public sector exclude banking, administration and defense, and other services. In addition, the estimates do not take into account social returns.

Table 2.12. Real Rates of Return to Investment
(In percent a year)

Period	Whole Public Sector	Public Sector Manufacturing	Private Sector Manufacturing
1960/61–1975/76	4.0–5.4	0.1–2.1	7.1–11.1
1976/77–1986/87	3.3–6.2	3.1–5.2	16.7–22.6

Source: Joshi and Little (1994), p. 325.

Joshi and Little offer several reasons for the apparent increase in growth and the efficiency of private sector investment in the second period. To some extent, greater aggregate demand pressures accounted for higher growth rates and also increased the returns to investment. More significantly, public investment increased, especially public infrastructure investment, which in turn may have contributed to the productivity of both public and private investment by reducing the problems of bottlenecks in the supply of power, transport, and communications. In addition, reforms begun in the late 1970s incorporating limited liberalization of industrial, trade, financial, and tax policies probably accounted for some of the improvement in efficiency.

III   The Adjustment Program of 1991/92 and Its Initial Results

Ajai Chopra and Charles Collyns

By the end of the 1980s, macroeconomic fundamentals in India were seriously deficient, leaving the country vulnerable to both domestic and external shocks. The deterioration in the fiscal accounts that began in the first half of the decade was not corrected, leading to a worsening of the external current account deficit. These internal and external imbalances were accompanied by large-scale borrowing, and both public and external debt accumulated rapidly. With much of the new debt on commercial terms, the debt-service burden increased substantially. The impact of the macroeconomic imbalances was exacerbated by the continued rigidities and distortions in the economy.

Thus, there was little to cushion the adverse effects of the 1990 disruptions in the Middle East that led to a sharp—albeit temporary—increase in the cost of imported oil and loss of workers' remittances. Concerns about the deteriorating external position and domestic political tensions caused a downgrading of India's international credit rating, and access to external commercial borrowing almost ceased by mid-1990. Combined with large outflows of nonresident deposits, the result was a major foreign exchange crisis that brought India to the brink of default in early 1991. Usable foreign exchange reserves were negligible, and the authorities were able to maintain debt-service payments only through a severe administrative squeeze on imports and the provision of emergency financing by the IMF.

The Stabilization and Adjustment Strategy

The adjustment strategy adopted in mid-1991 contained four major elements: (1) immediate stabilization measures, notably a 19 percent devaluation of the rupee and increases in interest rates, designed to restore confidence and reverse the short-term capital outflow; (2) fiscal consolidation aimed at reducing the central government deficit from about $8^1/_2$ percent of GDP in 1990/91 to 5 percent in 1992/93; (3) the mobilization of substantial exceptional financing from the IMF, the World Bank, and bilateral donors

to maintain a minimum level of imports; and (4) the initiation of major structural reforms. The early emphasis of the reforms was on industrial deregulation and trade liberalization, in a push to reduce drastically licensing requirements for investment and imports. Subsequently, the focus turned to tax reform, further trade liberalization (including reduction in tariffs), and financial sector reforms.

The magnitude of external effects and some rough measures of performance outcomes can be estimated using the approach developed by McCarthy, Neary, and Zanalda (1994). The first step involves estimating the effects on the balance of payments of three kinds of shocks—changes in the trade-weighted terms of trade, changes in global demand, and changes in international interest rates affecting debt-service payments.[1] Second, the economy's response to these shocks is disaggregated into various measures of adjustment: through expenditure switching (that is, changes in export performance and the degrees of import intensity) and through demand squeezes affecting economic activity.[2] Third, the need for additional net external financing is calculated as the difference between the effect of all shocks and policy responses. Responses are evaluated in terms of deviations from historical trends and obviously cannot be attributed to changes in policies

---

[1] The terms of trade shock is measured as the net import effect, that is, the change in export prices multiplied by the export volume minus the change in import prices multiplied by the import volume. The interest rate effect is calculated as the change in world interest rates (approximated by the London interbank offered rate) multiplied by the estimated stock of interest-sensitive external debt. Finally, the impact of changes in global demand is calculated as the deviation of the growth of world export volume from its estimated trend multiplied by the initial volume of Indian exports.

[2] Changes in export performance are measured as the initial export volume multiplied by the excess of actual export volume growth over world export volume growth. Changes in import intensity are calculated as the difference between import volumes expected on the assumption of historical import elasticity of GDP and actual import volumes. The import adjustment induced by the demand squeeze is calculated as the difference between import volumes expected on the assumption of historical import elasticity of GDP using the trend GDP growth rate versus the actual GDP growth rate.

alone since other factors would also have been at work, including indirect effects of the shocks themselves on the balance of payments through their impact on income and wealth. Nevertheless, in the absence of a fully specified and estimated model, these measures do provide useful summary indicators of the economy's response to external shocks.

Based on the approach of McCarthy, Neary, and Zanalda (1994), the negative terms of trade shock in 1990 amounted to over 1 percent of GDP, while the effect of changes in global demand and world interest rates were negligible. As noted above, this external shock acted as a trigger for the 1990–91 crisis, rather than being the fundamental cause. The initial 1990 adjustment to the external shock and the sharply reduced availability of external financing was achieved through a temporary administrative squeeze on imports. Subsequently, in 1991 the rupee was devalued and fiscal and monetary policies were tightened. As these policies took hold, the import restrictions were relaxed in March 1992. The tightening of import restrictions and the sharp depreciation of the rupee brought about a change in import intensity equivalent to over 1½ percent of GDP in 1991 (Chart 3.1, top panel).[3] In addition, export market shares rose markedly in 1993 and 1994 as a result of the depreciation of the real exchange rate and a reduction in the antiexport bias as the exchange and trade regime was liberalized. Thus, expenditure switching played a major role in the adjustment process.

The fiscal retrenchment and the tightening of monetary conditions undertaken as a part of the adjustment program led to a squeeze in domestic demand, which fell by 2½ percent in 1991/92 (Table 3.1 and Chart 3.1, middle panel).[4] Combined with the withdrawal of external financing and the constraints on imports (which fell heavily on intermediate inputs), this contributed to a downturn in growth. The constraints on external financing, however, eased considerably after 1991 (Chart 3.1, bottom panel). Combined with the demand stimulus arising from a widening of the fiscal deficit in 1993/94 and buoyant export growth, this surge helped generate a broad-based economic recovery.[5] On the supply side, industrial deregulation and trade liberalization contributed to the strong positive response.

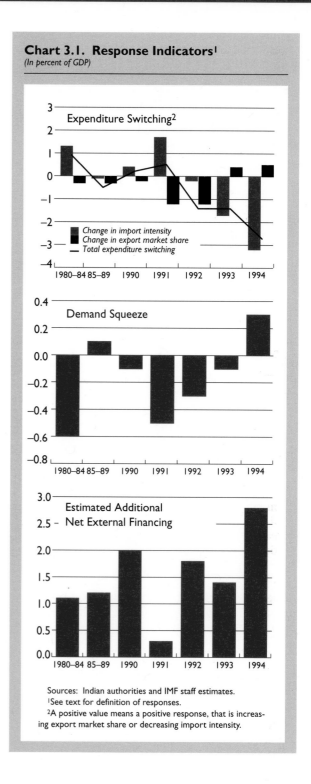

Chart 3.1. Response Indicators[1]
(In percent of GDP)

Sources: Indian authorities and IMF staff estimates.
[1]See text for definition of responses.
[2]A positive value means a positive response, that is increasing export market share or decreasing import intensity.

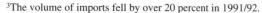

[3]The volume of imports fell by over 20 percent in 1991/92.

[4]The growth of consumption expenditures slowed to about 1½ percent a year in 1991/92 and 1992/93. Gross fixed investment also declined by 4 percent in 1991/92 followed by slow growth in the next two years. The decline in fixed investment in 1991/92 was accompanied by a sharp decline in stock building, resulting in a deeper fall in gross domestic capital formation.

[5]Both government consumption and public investment in 1993/94 grew at rates similar to those achieved in the 1980s, with the result that domestic demand grew by 3 percent.

The Response to the Reforms

Output performance since the implementation of the 1991 adjustment and reform program has had three noteworthy aspects:

Table 3.1. Domestic Demand
(Percent change in real terms)

	Average 1981/82– 1990/91	1989/90	1990/91	1991/92	1992/93	1993/94
Total consumption expenditure	4.9	4.6	3.7	1.4	1.6	4.5
Private final consumption expenditure	4.6	4.4	3.8	1.8	1.4	4.0
Government final consumption expenditure	7.2	5.6	3.3	–0.5	3.3	7.7
Gross domestic capital formation[1]	7.4	4.7	16.3	–14.2	–1.2	–2.4
Gross fixed capital formation	6.9	8.7	9.9	–4.0	1.6	3.8
Private	8.0	15.5	13.6	–8.0	8.6	2.6
Corporate	12.3	15.6	22.3	48.9	11.8	29.7
Household	8.6	15.4	10.0	–34.8	5.2	–28.4
Public	6.0	0.6	4.8	2.0	–7.9	5.6
Change in stocks[2]	2.7	2.1	3.1	0.8	2.1	0.4
Errors and omissions[2]	–0.8	0.7	1.4	0.7	–1.3	–0.9
Domestic demand[1]	5.4	4.6	6.7	–2.5	1.0	3.0
Memorandum items:						
Gross domestic capital formation[3]	7.7	2.1	1.37	–12.4	8.0	–3.9
GDP (at market prices)	5.9	6.6	5.7	0.5	4.6	3.5
GDP (at factor cost)	5.7	6.9	5.4	0.9	4.3	4.3

Source: Government of India, *National Account Statistics*, 1994.
[1]Including errors and omissions.
[2]Contributions to GDP growth.
[3]Excluding errors and omissions.

First, the initial impact on output of the stabilization measures taken in response to the crisis was fairly modest. Economic growth slowed to 1 percent in 1991/92, before rebounding to nearly 4$\frac{1}{2}$ percent a year in the following two years. A time-series analysis of potential GDP and output gaps indicates that the 1991–93 recession was considerably milder than previous recessions.[6] Over the last 35 years, India has had three severe recessions (1965–67, 1972–74, and 1979–82) with output gaps of more than 4$\frac{1}{2}$ percent of potential GDP (Chart 3.2). By contrast, the gap was less than 2 percent in 1991–93.

Second, notwithstanding favorable monsoons, the recovery following the stabilization program took time in gathering momentum. After the slowdown in growth in 1991/92, there were signs of a recovery beginning around the first quarter of 1992/93. However, this incipient recovery stalled toward the end of that year, and economic activity was again lackluster until about the third quarter of 1993/94. This pattern was particularly striking for industrial output, private fixed investment, and stock building. Third, beginning in late-1993 economic growth gathered substantial momentum across the board and is estimated to have reached nearly 6$\frac{1}{4}$ percent in 1994/95, three years after the launching of reforms. Investment appears particularly strong, and output in most sectors is increasing rapidly.

Against this background, this section looks at how sectoral performance has been affected by the combination of macroeconomic and structural measures. It must be emphasized, however, that interpreting the output and investment response to the reform program is complicated by the lack of data on capacity utilization.[7] In addition, national accounts data for 1994/95 are not yet available and information on

---

[6]Potential GDP was estimated using a filter developed by Hodrick and Prescott (1980). This filter defines a trend γ_t for the series y_t, which minimizes the weighted sum of two components: the squared distance between γ_t and y_t, and the squared distance between γ_t and γ_{t-1}, with a weight of $\lambda = 100$ commonly used for the second component when annual data are used.

[7]The substantial shifts in relative prices implied by the reforms may have made a significant part of existing capacity obsolete. A recent study by the Industrial Credit and Investment Corporation of India Limited (1994) indicates that capacity utilization dropped in 1991/92 and 1992/93, the latest period for which data are available. The study identifies a decline in demand (measured in terms of the growth of real sales) as the main reason for the initial decline in capacity utilization. Business surveys suggest that capacity utilization has increased somewhat since 1992/93, and these surveys cite plant capacity as an important constraint on production. Detailed information on capacity utilization is also compiled by the Central Statistical Organization, but is available with a considerable lag and only for a limited sample of industries.

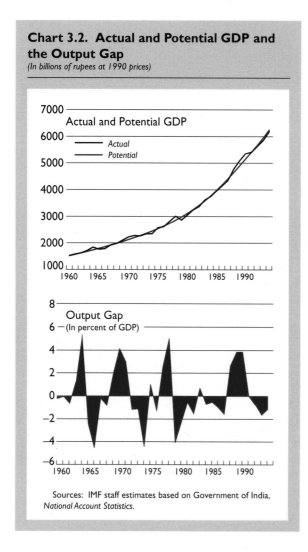

Chart 3.2. Actual and Potential GDP and the Output Gap
(In billions of rupees at 1990 prices)

Sources: IMF staff estimates based on Government of India, *National Account Statistics.*

a range of other variables (for example, employment and performance across regions) is sketchy or nonexistent. Furthermore, questions can be raised about the reliability of even the aggregate demand and output data that are available.

The Supply Side and Sectoral Performance

Within the overall growth picture since the 1991/92 crisis, sectoral performance has diverged markedly, with industrial growth falling well below long-term trends while agriculture and services grew more steadily. Industry contracted in 1991/92, and then rose by only 3.5 percent a year in the following two years, well below the 7.2 percent annual growth achieved during the 1980s (Table 3.2 and Chart 3.3). Since late 1993/94, however, industry has recovered broadly, with output estimated to have increased by about 8 percent in 1994/95. By contrast, the agricul-

tural sector has grown at close to its trend rate of the 1980s after a poor year in 1991/92.[8]

Several factors had a depressive effect on the industrial sector in 1991/92–1992/93. On the supply side, measures to restrict imports imposed in 1990/91 affected the availability of raw materials, spare parts and components, and capital goods that were important for a number of import-dependent manufacturing industries. In addition, tighter credit conditions affected the availability and cost of finance, especially working capital.

Total domestic demand was weak in 1991/92–1992/93 (see Table 3.1), owing to slow growth of agricultural output and incomes, a reduction in public expenditures, and sluggish private investment. Sales of manufactured goods were affected by weaker external demand because of the recession in member countries of the Organization for Economic Cooperation and Development (OECD) and the collapse of export markets in the former Soviet Union.

The adverse supply-side factors that contributed to a contraction in industrial output in 1991/92 were largely removed by the end of that year. Indeed, the industrial deregulation and trade liberalization made imported inputs cheaper and more accessible for industry, thus removing a major constraint on the supply side. Although industrial growth started to pick up in 1992/93, it continued to be constrained by weak demand. In addition, temporary setbacks in 1992 and 1993 had an impact on confidence, thus affecting business plans and expectations. First, the stock market scam uncovered in May 1992 affected liquidity and temporarily affected investor confidence. Second, and perhaps more important, riots and other civil disturbances in the period December 1992 to March 1993 led to considerable sociopolitical uncertainty that affected industrial production. Thus, the growth of industrial output continued to be weak for much of 1993/94.

There is ample evidence of a broad-based recovery of the industrial sector in 1994/95. The capital goods sector, which had suffered a sharp recession for three years, bounced back vigorously. The production of capital goods in 1994/95 was a remarkable 24 percent higher than the previous year (Table 3.3), suggesting a pickup in investment in new machinery to install fresh capacity. The initial decline in capital goods production in 1991/92–1993/94 was related mainly to the weakness of domestic investment demand, particularly by the public sector. Contrary to the concerns that had been expressed, the liberalization of capital goods imports does not seem to have had a strong impact on the domestic capital

---

[8]The decline in agricultural production in 1991/92 can be ascribed in large part to an erratic monsoon that year that led to a 4.5 percent fall in food grain production.

Table 3.2. GDP by Sector of Production
(Percent change)

	Average 1981/82– 1990/91	1990/91	1991/92	1992/93	1993/94	Est. 1994/95
GDP (factor cost)	5.7	5.4	0.9	4.3	4.3	6.2
Agriculture	3.5	3.8	−2.5	5.3	2.9	4.8
Industry	7.2	6.6	−0.8	3.5	3.5	7.4
Services	6.4	4.4	5.4	4.9	5.9	6.1

Source: Government of India, Central Statistical Organization.

goods industry as a whole.[9] Capital goods imports fell sharply in the initial adjustment year and stayed low in the following year as well (Table 3.4). Despite the sharp rebound in 1993/94, the ratio of capital goods imports to domestic value added still remained at around its level of 1990/91.

The consumer goods sector, which grew by less than 2 percent a year in 1991/92 and 1992/93, has also picked up markedly. The production of consumer durables was particularly hard hit by the demand squeeze in 1991/92, but by 1993/94 it had recovered strongly, in part because of substantial reductions in excise duties on automobiles and electronic goods in the budget for that year. Although

growth of the consumer durables sector slowed somewhat in 1994/95, possibly because of capacity constraints, this sector is likely to grow rapidly in the years ahead in view of major investments made possible by the end of licensing and the liberalization of foreign investment rules. For example, joint ventures have either been launched or are planned by a number of companies producing passenger cars and consumer entertainment electronics.

The production of consumer nondurables has also picked up in 1994/95.[10] In general, however, this sector has not registered particularly rapid growth. Data problems may have been the cause of the low recorded growth of this sector. For example, the index of industrial production does not provide good

[9]One concern was that the reduction of trade barriers would affect the capital goods sector in particular because the tariffs on finished capital goods were lowered by more than the tariffs on the inputs into the production of capital goods.

[10]The weak performance of this sector in 1993/94 reflected in part a sharp decline in sugar production due to a drop in sugarcane cultivation.

Chart 3.3 Industrial Production
(In percent)

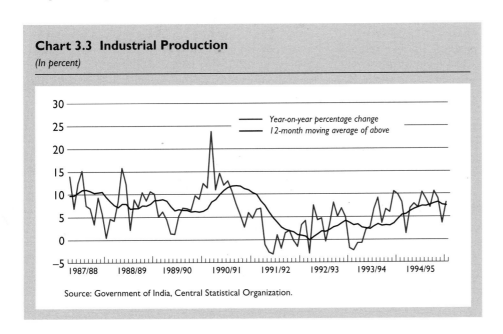

Source: Government of India, Central Statistical Organization.

Table 3.3. Index of Industrial Production
(Percent change)

	Average 1981/82– 1990/91	1990/91	1991/92	1992/93	1993/94	1994/95
Overall index	7.8	8.3	0.6	2.3	4.1	8.4
Capital goods	11.5	17.4	−8.6	−0.1	−5.3	24.0
Consumer goods	6.7	10.4	1.5	1.8	3.1	8.2
Consumer durables	13.0	14.8	−10.7	−0.7	15.2	9.5
Consumer nondurables	5.7	9.4	4.7	2.4	0.5	7.9
Basic goods	7.5	3.8	6.5	2.6	5.9	3.8
Intermediate goods	6.2	6.1	−2.2	5.4	11.4	4.4

Source: Government of India, Central Statistical Organization.

coverage of the small-scale sector. Thus, despite the strong export performance of textiles and garments, measured output in these sectors was stagnant.[11] The continued policy of reserving production of many consumer nondurables for small-scale industries is also likely to have restrained growth in this sector by restricting investment and perpetuating its greater difficulty in accessing financing and foreign expertise.

The production of basic goods has increased fairly steadily over the last three years. To a large extent, output in infrastructure sectors such as electricity, petroleum, and coal mining is determined by investment trends in earlier years and is therefore little affected by short-term fluctuations in aggregate demand. Moreover, any supply response to the liberalization that has occurred will only be evident after a substantial lag given the long gestation period of projects in this sector. However, there has not yet been much new investment in this sector largely because frameworks for investment in areas such as power and hydrocar-

bons have been delayed. The lack of adequate infrastructure may prevent industry from committing itself to major investments in a number of other areas as well. Uncertainty about the policy framework, as demonstrated by marked shifts in the policy on subsidies, has also inhibited investment in the fertilizer industry.

Among the nonindustrial sectors of the economy, agriculture has benefited from good monsoons after 1991/92. Nevertheless, growth in output of the major food grains has been relatively slow. The increased procurement prices and some relaxation of constraints on exports of high-value grains should have increased production incentives. However, the pattern of input costs remains highly distorted and cutbacks in public spending on agricultural infrastructure are apparently having a negative impact on growth. More positively, partial liberalization of restrictions on internal and external trade and improved technologies have encouraged rapid growth in high value-added products such as fruits and vegetables, cut flowers, and marine products, and exports have grown rapidly, although the total amounts remain small.

The services sector has consistently outperformed the rest of the economy in recent years, and by a wider margin than in the 1980s. Services have clearly benefited from a relatively high marginal propensity to consume. Moreover, technological advances have made it possible for India to compete on a global basis in areas such as software development and information services. Reduced restrictions on private sector involvement have also played an important part, and indeed the response to liberalization has probably been quicker than in other sectors, partly because of lower fixed-investment requirements. A good example is the very rapid

---

[11]Analysis of production trends for other categories is also complicated by weaknesses in the statistics. The present index of industrial production has not been rebased since 1980/81 and does not necessarily capture the substantial changes in India's industrial structure since then. Many fast-growing sectors such as automobiles, electronics, and computers are substantially underrepresented in the index. A second difficulty is that the index is based largely on information from the registered sector, while nearly half of output from Indian manufacturing is in the small-scale and village sectors. Little comprehensive information is available on how the informal sector has fared in recent years, although some industries—such as garments—seem to have done particularly well. Third, with the dismantling of the industrial licensing system in August 1991, the response rate may well have deteriorated as the incentives for prompt and accurate reporting have been reduced.

Table 3.4. Capital Goods Sector
(In millions of U.S. dollars)

	1989/90	1990/91	1991/92	1992/93	1993/94
Capital goods imports	5,287.0	5,833.0	4,233.0	4,531.0	6,040.2
Metal products	148.0	168.0	130.0	146.0	175.9
Nonelectrical machinery	2,084.0	2,363.0	1,631.0	1,819.0	2,401.9
Electrical machinery	1,121.0	949.0	630.0	826.0	794.4
Transport equipment	891.0	931.0	371.0	462.0	1,267.0
Project goods	1,043.0	1,422.0	1,471.0	1,278.0	1,401.0
Domestic value added[1]	8,040.6	9,492.7	9,105.7	9,472.6	9,755.1
Metal products	904.7	959.2	909.9	892.9	933.6
Nonelectrical machinery	2,305.3	2,646.2	2,647.8	2,728.4	2,874.9
Electrical machinery	2,684.1	3,477.8	3,107.5	3,176.1	3,037.1
Transport equipment	2,146.5	2,409.5	2,440.5	2,675.2	2,909.5
Ratio of imports to value added	65.8	61.4	46.5	47.8	61.9
Metal products	16.4	17.5	14.3	16.4	18.8
Nonelectrical machinery	90.4	89.3	61.6	66.7	83.5
Electrical machinery	41.8	27.3	20.3	26.0	26.2
Transport equipment	41.5	38.6	15.2	17.3	43.5

Sources: Indian authorities; and IMF staff estimates.

[1]Estimated from value-added data in 1989/90, industrial production information, and import unit value index for capital imports.

growth of passengers carried on private airlines since the opening up of this sector in 1992. There has also been substantial change in the financial services industry following liberalization in this sector, including the expansion of the mutual fund and investment banking sectors and the entry of private banks, although large parts of the retail banking and insurance sectors remain dominated by the public sector.

Regional Patterns

Growth across states varied considerably during the 1980s, with Andhra Pradesh, Gujarat, Haryana, Maharashtra, and Punjab achieving relatively high per capita income growth, while per capita income in other highly populated states such as Bihar, Orissa, Uttar Pradesh, and West Bengal was well below the national average (Table 3.5).[12] Preliminary data indicate that these differences are likely to have been maintained if not accentuated

[12]Cashin and Sahay (1995) examine the determinants of growth for 20 Indian states during 1961–91, using cross-sectional estimation and the analytical framework of the neoclassical growth model. They find evidence of absolute convergence, but at a very slow rate of 1.5 percent a year, which is substantially below convergence rates found across regions in industrial countries. This implies that in the Indian context it would take about 45 years to close half of the gap between any state's initial per capita income and the steady-state per capita income.

since 1991/92. Although data on growth performance across states are only available with a considerable lag, information on the statewise distribution of new investment from memorandums of investment intention shows that 60 percent of new investment since 1991 has been located in only four states representing 37 percent of the population: Gujarat, Maharashtra, Tamil Nadu, and Uttar Pradesh. (Comparable figures prior to 1991 are not available.) Approvals for foreign direct investment have also been quite heavily concentrated with over half of approvals being directed at four states (Delhi, Gujarat, Maharashtra, and West Bengal).

The marked differences across regions are not surprising for two reasons. First, the previous licensing system that tried to allocate investment across states has been dismantled. Thus, new investment is likely to flow to states that offer a more hospitable environment. Second, states such as Maharashtra and Gujarat have lighter, more dynamic industries that are primarily in private hands. These states are therefore better placed to take advantage of the new policies not only because they are richer but also because of their greater outward orientation. By contrast, states such as Bihar and Orissa are better endowed with natural resources such as iron ore and coal, and hence are the base of heavy public sector industries, which have not yet benefited from the reform process.

Table 3.5. Per Capita State Domestic Product
(In 1970/71 rupees)

	1970/71	1980/81	1990/91	Average Annual Growth Rate (In percent)		
				1970–80	1980–90	1970–90
Andhra Pradesh	585	603	926	0.3	4.4	2.3
Arunachal Pradesh	456	682	987	4.1	3.8	3.9
Assam	535	524	769	−0.2	3.9	1.8
Bihar	402	401	519	—	2.6	1.3
Delhi	1,199	1,642	2,082	3.2	2.4	2.8
Goa	915	1,373	1,544	4.1	1.2	2.7
Gujarat	829	851	1,145	0.3	3.0	1.6
Haryana	877	1,035	1,471	1.7	3.6	2.6
Himachal Pradesh	651	744	937	1.3	2.3	1.8
Jammu and Kashmir	548	776	758	3.5	−0.2	1.6
Karnataka	641	667	906	0.4	3.1	1.7
Kerala	594	659	789	1.0	1.8	1.4
Madhya Pradesh	484	582	787	1.9	3.1	2.5
Maharashtra	783	1,060	1,487	3.1	3.4	3.3
Manipur	390	624	762	4.8	2.0	3.4
Nagaland	489	632	974	2.6	4.4	3.5
Orissa	485	538	704	1.0	2.7	1.9
Punjab	1,070	1,168	1,648	0.9	3.5	2.2
Rajasthan	645	534	790	−1.9	4.0	1.0
Tamil Nadu	581	654	904	1.2	3.3	2.2
Tripura	502	578	698	1.4	1.9	1.7
Uttar Pradesh	486	558	696	1.4	2.2	1.8
West Bengal	722	704	938	−0.3	2.9	1.3

Source: Ministry of Finance (1995).

Table 3.6 Unemployment Trends[1]
(In percent)

	Male				Female			
	Urban		Rural		Urban		Rural	
	Usual status "adjusted"	Weekly status	Usual status "adjusted"	Weekly status	Usual status "adjusted"	Weekly status	Usual status "adjusted"	Weekly status
Post-reform period								
1992	4.3	4.6	1.2	2.2	5.8	6.2	0.6	1.2
1991 (July–Dec.)	4.1	4.8	1.6	2.2	4.3	5.6	0.7	1.2
Pre-reform period								
1990/91	4.5	5.1	1.1	2.2	4.7	5.3	0.3	2.1
1989/90	3.9	4.5	1.3	2.6	2.7	4.0	0.6	2.1
1987/88	5.2	6.6	1.8	4.2	6.2	9.2	2.4	4.4

Source: Government of India, National Sample Surveys.
 [1]Usual status "adjusted" unemployment refers to persons who were not working but were seeking or available for work for more than half of the 365 days in the reference year, adjusted for those unemployed but working in a subsidiary capacity. Weekly status unemployment refers to persons who did not work for even one hour or any one day but were seeking or available for work at any time during the reference week.

Table 3.7. Percentage of Persons Below Poverty Line[1]

	Poverty Line (In rupees)		Poverty Ratio (In percent)		
	Rural	Urban	Rural	Urban	Combined
1983	101.8	117.5	40.4	28.1	37.4
Number of poor (in millions)			221.5	49.5	271.0
1987/88	131.8	152.1	33.4	20.1	29.9
Number of poor (in millions)			196.0	41.7	237.7
1988/89	142.5	164.1	22.5	14.2	20.4
Number of poor (in millions)			136.6	29.1	165.5
1989/90	152.5	170.1	20.3	13.3	18.5
Number of poor (in millions)			125.2	28.0	153.2
1990/91	169.6	195.0	19.7	10.8	17.4
Number of poor (in millions)			123.6	23.4	147.0
1991 July–Dec.	191.2	220.7	20.5	12.9	18.5
Number of poor (in millions)			130.3	29.0	159.3
1992 Jan.–Dec.	210.4	242.8	22.9	13.0	20.3
Number of poor (in millions)			147.6	29.5	177.2

Source: Planning Commission.

[1]The poverty estimates up to 1987–88 are based on the quinquennial national sample surveys, whereas the poverty estimates for 1988–89 to 1992 are based on "thin samples" each year with sample size of about one fifth of the detailed quinquennial surveys. The results of these "thin samples" must therefore be interpreted with caution when assessing trends in poverty over time.

The Impact on Unemployment and Poverty

Official estimates indicate that total economywide employment increased by an average of 5 million a year in the second half of the 1980s. In the crisis year of 1991/92, employment increased by only 3 million (that is, less than 1 percent). The pace of job creation has picked up since then, with the increase in employment averaging 6.3 million a year during 1992/93–1994/95. As employment in the organized sector has been essentially flat, much of the increased employment has been in the informal sector. National Sample Surveys for 1991 (July–December) and 1992 (full year), the most recent period for which surveys are available, suggest that there was no discernable change in unemployment in the first 18 months after the initiation of the adjustment and reform program (Table 3.6).[13] Indeed, contrary to the expectation that the reforms might have led to an in-

crease in urban unemployment, the data suggest that urban unemployment for males (who account for the bulk of urban jobs) actually declined marginally.[14]

Official estimates based on the latest survey data also indicate that the proportion of the population that is below the poverty line rose somewhat in the initial adjustment period. This ratio increased from 19.7 percent in 1990/91 to nearly 22.9 percent in 1992 in the rural sector; there was also a rise—from 10.8 percent to 13.0 percent—in the urban sector (Table 3.7). The marked increase in rural poverty is likely to have been largely related to the cyclical decline in agricultural production in 1991/92, rather than any structural shift.[15]

[13]Unemployment data for India need to be treated with caution as there is considerable underemployment.

[14]Although India's rigid labor laws likely prevented some unemployment, these laws cover only the organized sector, which is just 8 percent of the labor force. Thus, even if large-scale layoffs were possible in the organized sector it is unlikely that the overall picture would be dramatically altered.

[15]The 1992 National Sample Survey data are based on a smaller than normal sample of 12,000 to 15,000 households and are hence not deemed reliable enough for assessing trends in poverty over time. A broader survey of 100,000 households was conducted in 1993/94 and the results are being compiled.

IV   The Behavior of Private Investment

Karen Parker

As the results of the growth accounting exercise in Section II indicate, capital accumulation has been the main impetus to growth in India over the past thirty years. Gross domestic capital formation nearly tripled as a share of GDP from 1950/51 to 1990/91 (Chart 4.1). The increase in domestic capital formation can be attributed in part to public sector investment, which rose from 3 percent of GDP in the mid-1950s to over 10 percent by the mid-1980s. However, about two thirds of gross capital formation has been undertaken by the private sector, and the latter's contribution is likely to increase over the next decade. To understand India's growth record and prospects, it is therefore important to understand the factors that underlie private investment behavior.

This section analyzes the determinants of private investment in India, focusing in particular on its behavior since the reform program was launched in 1991. The econometric results suggest that macroeconomic policies have played an important role—both direct and indirect—in determining the behavior of private investment over the past twenty years. Both the cost and availability of credit to the private sector, as well as public sector investment, have had a significant impact on private capital formation. Private investment has also been influenced by the behavior of industrial production and by the presence of price uncertainty.

Private capital formation relative to GDP fell sharply during 1991/92–1993/94 (Table 4.1). Much of the decline resulted from lower household investment in machinery and equipment; household and corporate inventories also fell relative to GDP during this period.[1] In contrast, corporate fixed investment is estimated to have risen by 4 percentage points of GDP from 1990/91 to 1993/94. The model suggests that a tightening of financial conditions and heightened uncertainty led to the initial sharp decline in investment. Despite the easing of credit conditions in 1992/93–1993/94, gross capital formation continued to decline as a result of weak domestic demand and persistent uncertainty.

While severe, India's "investment pause" appears to have been relatively brief. The upturn in production in the capital goods sector and the surge in capital goods imports point to a robust recovery of investment in 1994/95. Based on the econometric results, private capital formation is projected to have recovered to $13\frac{1}{2}$ percent of GDP in 1994/95 and to rise further to almost 16 percent of GDP by 1995/96. Underlying the investment recovery is an acceleration of industrial growth, improved corporate profitability resulting from business and financial restructuring, and diminished uncertainty.

A Model of Private Investment Behavior

This study uses a general-to-specific modeling approach to identify the principal determinants of private capital formation in India.[2] A large set of explanatory variables was narrowed to seven through the successive elimination of statistically insignificant terms. All variables were expressed in scaled form or as rates of change to avoid potentially spurious correlation among nonstationary series.[3] Regressions on annual data were estimated using ordinary least squares, and heteroskedasticity-consistent standard errors were computed.

The choice of the set of potential explanatory variables reflects recent developments in the literature on investment (for a survey of recent empirical work, see Rama (1993) and Greene and Villanueva (1991)). Neoclassical accelerator and "Tobin's Q" models have been augmented to allow for the effects

---

[1]Household investment includes capital formation in the informal sector, that is, firms employing fewer than ten persons. However, large errors and omissions in the national accounts statistics make it difficult to interpret sectoral patterns of investment. Joshi and Little (1994) raise doubts about the split between corporate and household investment in India.

[2]The methodology used is similar to that in Goldsbrough and others (forthcoming).

[3]Augmented Dickey-Fuller tests did not support the hypothesis of a unit root in any series except public and private investment. However, these tests are known to have low power in small samples. An analysis of the sample autocorrelation functions for all of the series revealed low or rapidly decaying values.

Chart 4.1 Gross Domestic Capital Formation
(In percent of GDP at current prices)

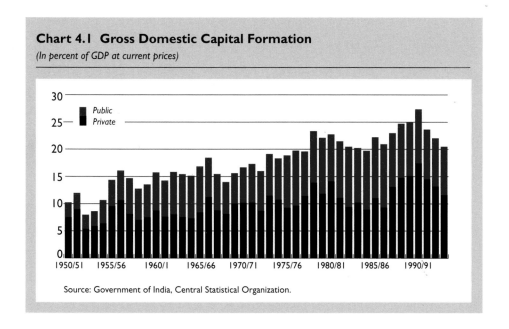

Source: Government of India, Central Statistical Organization.

of credit rationing, external financing constraints, and uncertainty. The initial set of variables for India included the growth of real GDP and of industrial production (lagged one and two periods to avoid simultaneity bias); the real weighted average lending rate; the growth of real credit to the private sector from banks and term lending institutions; the share of public investment in GDP; the level of foreign exchange reserves (in months of imports); external debt service (in months of exports); and the variance of monthly inflation, the real exchange rate, and the index of industrial production (as proxies for uncertainty). A description of the initial set of variables is given in the Appendix.

Table 4.2 presents the final estimation results, while Table 4.3 indicates the contribution of each of the explanatory variables. The real lending rate was found to be a significant determinant of private investment in India, with the expected sign. The real growth of credit was also significant and had the correct sign.[4] Both the price and quantity of credit have a bearing on investment, which suggests that the Indian credit markets were segmented during the period under study; some borrowers may have

[4]The real interest rate and the real growth of credit are highly correlated, due to the influence of their common deflator, the wholesale price index.

Table 4.1. Private Capital Formation
(In percent of GDP at constant prices)

	1989/90	1990/91	1991/92	1992/93	1993/94
Private fixed investment	11.8	12.7	11.6	12.1	12.0
Corporate	3.5	4.1	6.0	6.4	8.1
Household	8.3	8.6	5.6	5.6	3.9
Changes in private stocks	1.6	2.5	1.2	1.6	–0.1
Corporate	1.1	0.9	0.4	0.9	–0.4
Household	0.5	1.5	0.7	0.7	0.3
Errors and omissions	0.7	1.3	0.7	–1.2	0.8
Private capital formation	13.4	15.2	12.8	13.7	11.9
(Including errors and omissions)	14.1	16.5	13.5	12.5	11.0

Source: Data provided by the Indian authorities.

Table 4.2. Private Investment Equation[1]

$$
\begin{aligned}
\text{LIPE} = \;& -15.35 \;-\; 1.26\,\text{RWGT} \;+\; 1.22\,\text{RCRE} \;-\; 1.72\,\text{LIG} \;-\; 128.17\,\text{VREER} \\
& (-5.58)\quad(-2.50)\qquad\quad(2.15)\qquad\quad(-4.46)\qquad\quad(-2.74) \\[4pt]
& -\;823.47\,\text{VINFL} \;+\; 0.52\,\text{LIPE}(-1) \;+\; 2.00\,\text{IIPGR}(-1) \;+\; 1.80\,\text{IIPGR}(-2) \\
& (-4.21)\qquad\qquad(4.05)\qquad\qquad(2.45)\qquad\qquad(2.90)
\end{aligned}
$$

R-squared	0.79
Adjusted R-squared	0.65
Standard error of regression	0.11
Durbin's *h*-statistic	−1.82
Jarque-Bera	0.45
Arch	0.30
White	1.05

Source: IMF staff estimates.

[1]Estimated using annual data and ordinary least squares, with heteroskedasticity-consistent standard errors. Estimation period: 1973/74–1993/94. *T*-statistics are given in parentheses. A description of the variables is given in the Appendix.

Table 4.3. Investment Equation—Decomposition of Estimated Change
(Dependent variable: Gross private investment/GDP, constant prices, in logs; OLS estimates, 1973/74–1993/94)

Explanatory Variable	1980/81–1986/87		1986/87–1990/91		1990/91–1993/94	
	Estimated change in I/GDP (In percent of GDP)	Share of estimated change explained by	Estimated change in I/GDP (In percent of GDP)	Share of estimated change explained by	Estimated change in I/GDP (In percent of GDP)	Share of estimated change explained by
Real lending rate	−1.6	43.6	1.1	26.2	−0.2	10.0
Real growth of credit to the private sector	0.8	−22.5	−1.2	−30.0	−0.4	17.4
Ratio of public investment to GDP (constant prices)	−4.6	127.9	3.6	86.5	1.8	−76.3
Variance of monthly changes in REER	0.03	−0.8	−0.7	−16.5	0.5	−22.4
Variance of monthly changes in inflation	0.08	−2.1	−0.2	−5.4	0.2	−10.0
Lagged dependent variable	−0.9	24.0	1.9	45.3	−0.8	34.6
Lagged growth of industrial production (1 period)	2.3	−64.3	−0.2	−4.6	−1.7	68.8
Lagged growth of industrial production (2 periods)	0.2	−5.7	−0.1	−1.5	−1.9	77.9
Total	−3.6	100.0	4.1	100.0	−2.4	100.0
	1980/81–1986/87		1986/87–1990/91		1990/91–1993/94	
Memorandum items:						
Actual change in the dependent variable (in percent of GDP)	−5.4		7.7		−5.4	
Share of actual change in the dependent variable explained by regression equation	66.7		53.2		44.4	
Share of actual change in the dependent variable due to change in residual	33.3		46.8		55.5	

Source: IMF staff estimates.

experienced credit rationing in the repressed segments of the market. Over the next several years, deregulation and heightened competition would be expected to increase the influence of interest rates—and decrease that of credit—as determinants of private investment.

The growth of industrial production lagged one and two periods (a proxy for aggregate demand) was positively correlated with private capital formation, consistent with conventional "flexible-accelerator" models of investment behavior. What is striking is the long lag with which industrial performance influences investment. This may reflect the rigidities associated with industrial licensing, trade, and exchange controls in the pre-reform period.

Public sector investment is estimated to have had a negative impact on private capital formation in India. When public investment was separated into its infrastructure and noninfrastructure components, both terms bore negative signs, although the infrastructure variable was not statistically significant.[5] These results are robust to alternative lag structures. The fact that the public investment variable is significant in a regression that includes both real interest rates and credit suggests that there has been competition between the public and private sectors for physical as well as financial resources. These results are consistent with earlier research that finds more evidence of crowding out than complementarity in public and private investment in India (see Sundararajan and Thakur (1980) and Pradhan, Ratha, and Sarma (1990)).[6]

Unlike some other developing countries in the 1980s, external financing constraints (proxied by the level of foreign exchange reserves and the debt-service ratio) do not appear to have had much impact on private investment in India. This is not surprising, since the economy was largely closed to international trade and capital flows until 1991. Indian investment has not been heavily import intensive. Moreover, although public sector debt is high relative to GDP, it comprises mostly domestic obligations.[7] India's external debt, at about 30 percent of GDP, has a large concessional element.

Both the variance of inflation and of the real exchange rate were negatively related to private investment, consistent with theories that emphasize the detrimental effects of price uncertainty on private

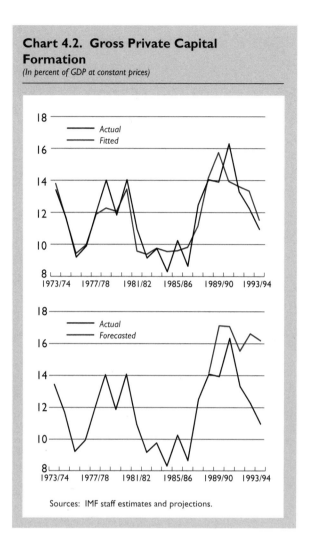

Chart 4.2. Gross Private Capital Formation
(In percent of GDP at constant prices)

Sources: IMF staff estimates and projections.

capital formation.[8] Uncertainty may also explain the long lags through which developments in the industrial sector influence investment. The variance of industrial production was not statistically significant.[9]

The explanatory power of the regression is reasonably high; actual and fitted values of the dependent variable are plotted in Chart 4.2 (upper panel). The equation passed a battery of tests for residual serial correlation, heteroskedasticity, and parameter instability. The model performs less well out of sample (Chart 4.2, lower panel), which is not surprising in light of the extensive changes in the structure of the

[5]Infrastructure investment includes investment in agriculture; electricity, gas, and water supply; and transportation, communication, and storage facilities.

[6]Using a pooled time-series, cross-section approach for a sample of 23 countries (including India), however, Greene and Villanueva (1991) found some evidence that public sector investment has been complementary to private investment.

[7]Of course, a large domestic debt burden can inhibit investment through crowding out, as discussed above.

[8]Dixit and Pindyck (1994) and others have persuasively shown why firms postpone irreversible investments when they are uncertain about changing economic conditions or the scope and duration of key policy reforms.

[9]Monthly interest rate data are not available to compute the variance of interest rates. In any event, such a term is unlikely to have been significant, given the stability of administered lending rates.

Table 4.4. Private Investment Forecast[1]

	1990/91	1991/92	1992/93	1993/94	1994/95
Explanatory variables					
Real credit growth (in percent)	1.0	—	8.1	−1.7	10.0
Real interest rate (in percent)	2.4	1.9	10.2	3.9	5.5
Government investment (in percent of GDP)	9.1	8.5	8.3	8.4	8.4
Growth of industrial production (−1)	7.9	8.7	—	1.4	4.7
Growth of industrial production (−2)	8.3	7.9	8.7	—	1.4
Variance of monthly inflation	0.00006	0.00006	0.00007	0.00004	0.00004
Variance of real exchange rate	0.00054	0.00250	0.00075	0.00021	0.00027
Lagged private investment (in percent of GDP)	13.9	16.3	13.3	12.3	10.9
Private investment (in percent of GDP)					
Predicted	13.9	13.6	13.3	11.5	13.6
Actual	16.3	13.3	12.3	10.9	...

Source: IMF staff estimates and projections.

[1]Predicted values based on parameter estimates for full sample period.

economy over the past five years.[10] For example, the parameter on the real interest rate variable was higher when estimated using the full sample period than when the data were truncated at 1988.[11] The parameter on industrial production was also higher, while those for public investment, lagged private investment, and the proxies for uncertainty were lower.

These results should be interpreted with caution, given the limited degrees of freedom afforded by the brief sample period. Moreover, this period witnessed important changes in the economy—particularly since the late 1980s—which make it difficult to assess the responsiveness of investment to changing economic conditions. Finally, the national accounts data may not be fully reliable.

The Response of Private Investment to Reforms

The behavior of investment in the post-reform period can be divided into three distinct phases: the crisis of 1991/92, when private capital formation contracted sharply; the period 1992/93–1993/94, in which investment remained sluggish despite an easing of financial conditions and an improved economic outlook; and the period 1994/95–1995/96, for

---

[10]To test the model's out-of-sample properties, the series were truncated at 1988 and the equation was re-estimated. The resulting parameter values were used to compute a dynamic private investment forecast.

[11]This is as one would expect, given the increased role of market forces in the allocation of credit. The parameter and t-statistic on the credit variable were correspondingly lower for the full sample period.

which there is evidence of a robust and broad-based investment recovery.

The Crisis of 1991/92

The initial decline in private capital formation can be attributed in large part to a sharp tightening of credit conditions beginning in 1990/91 (Table 4.4 and Chart 4.3, upper panel). Administered interest rates were increased, while the growth of base money was sharply curtailed; real Reserve Bank credit to the financial system declined by one third from 1989/90 to 1992/93.

As a result, real banking system credit to the private sector fell by 6 percent in 1990/91–1991/92. Even with higher lending from the term financing institutions, total credit remained flat during this period. Foreign sources of financing (especially nonresident deposits) also contracted as a result of the balance of payments crisis (Table 4.5). Total financing for private investment is estimated to have shrunk by a quarter in dollar terms between 1989/90 and 1991/92. Tighter financial conditions were exacerbated by the sizable currency depreciation and imposition of import controls, which raised the cost of imported inputs.

Medium-sized and large industrial borrowers bore the brunt of the credit squeeze (Chart 4.3, lower panels). Lending to the engineering sector—which had grown rapidly from the mid-1970s onward—was especially affected, as was credit to the textile industry. Lending to small-scale agriculture, agro-based industry, chemicals, and metals was less affected. Real interest rates responded with a lag to the tightening of financial conditions, rising to 10 percent in 1992/93 (Chart 4.4).

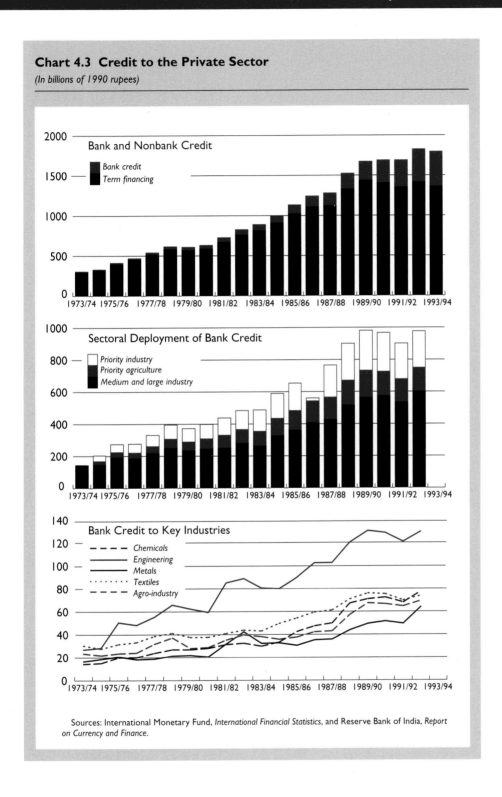

Chart 4.3 Credit to the Private Sector

(In billions of 1990 rupees)

Bank and Nonbank Credit

  Bank credit
  Term financing

Sectoral Deployment of Bank Credit

  Priority industry
  Priority agriculture
  Medium and large industry

Bank Credit to Key Industries

  Chemicals
  Engineering
  Metals
  Textiles
  Agro-industry

Sources: International Monetary Fund, *International Financial Statistics*, and Reserve Bank of India, *Report on Currency and Finance*.

The initial contraction of private investment would have been greater were it not for the reduction in the public sector's borrowing requirement, which alleviated some of the crowding-out effects discussed earlier. Cuts in capital expenditure reduced public sector investment by about ½ of 1 percent of GDP, continuing a trend decline that began in 1987/88 (Chart 4.5, upper panel).

Heightened uncertainty may also have played a role in the initial slowdown of investment. The

Table 4.5. Sources of Financing for Private Investment
(In millions of U.S. dollars)

	1985/86	1986/87	1987/88	1988/89	1989/90	1990/91	1991/92	1992/93	1993/94	Est. 1994/95
Domestic financing	11,736	11,395	10,665	19,212	19,485	16,095	14,433	18,985	17,298	28,395
Debt[1]	11,736	11,062	10,665	19,135	18,434	13,766	11,799	14,656	10,291	23,558
Commercial bank borrowing	9,473	8,082	7,734	14,886	12,182	7,640	5,743	6,830	4,254	16,146
Term lending from Indian financial institutions	1,567	1,763	2,414	2,804	3,123	4,482	4,321	4,420	3,097	3,912
Corporate debentures	696	1,217	517	1,445	3,129	1,644	1,735	3,406	2,940	3,500
Equity (new share issues)	—	333	—	77	1,051	2,329	2,634	4,329	7,007	4,837
Foreign financing	1,603	2,289	1,600	2,350	2,760	2,414	1,604	231	4,148	4,432
Debt	1,443	2,081	1,419	2,052	2,419	2,249	1,456	−358	38	182
Commercial borrowing	1,303	2,236	1,361	2,157	2,505	2,019	1,417	−392	−11	127
Private nonguaranteed	140	−155	58	−105	−86	230	39	34	49	55
Equity	160	208	181	298	341	165	148	589	4,110	4,250
Foreign direct investment	160	208	181	298	341	165	148	344	620	950
GDR issues	—	—	—	—	—	—	—	241	1,838	1,750
Investment by foreign institutional investors	—	—	—	—	—	—	—	4	1,652	1,550
Total	13,339	13,684	12,265	21,562	22,245	18,509	16,037	19,216	21,446	32,827

Sources: International Finance Corporation, Emerging Markets database; Reserve Bank of India, *Report on Currency and Finance*; International Monetary Fund, *International Financial Statistics*; Securities and Exchange Board of India; *Business Standard*; and IMF staff estimates.

[1]Computed as the net flow of credit in rupee terms, divided by the period average exchange rate. There were large valuation adjustments during 1988/89–1992/93.

variance of both inflation and the real exchange rate rose in 1990/91–1991/92, partly as a result of the sharp currency realignment that occurred during this period.

Chart 4.4 Real Interest Rates and Investment
(In percent)

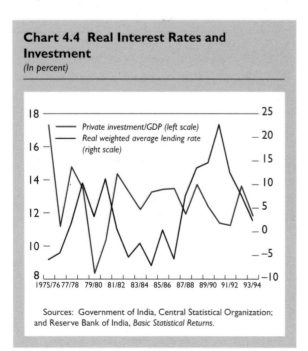

— Private investment/GDP (left scale)
— Real weighted average lending rate (right scale)

Sources: Government of India, Central Statistical Organization; and Reserve Bank of India, *Basic Statistical Returns*.

The "Investment Pause" of 1992/93–1993/94

Credit conditions eased considerably in 1992/93 and 1993/94. Reductions in banks' cash and statutory liquidity requirements (facilitated by further fiscal adjustment in 1992/93) released resources for private investment. Bank credit to the commercial sector recovered to precrisis levels, and term lending by Indian financial institutions expanded vigorously. The increase in the public sector borrowing requirement in 1993/94 was more than offset by a surge in private capital flows. Domestic and foreign equity investment increased dramatically, buoyed by recovery in the Indian capital markets and reform of the trade and investment regime. Real interest rates fell sharply.

Many firms used the opportunity created by India's increased access to foreign financing to restructure their balance sheets away from high-cost domestic debt in favor of domestic and foreign equity financing. In real terms, bank credit to the private sector contracted in 1993/94, even as overall financing for private investment continued to rise.

Nevertheless, the decline in gross capital formation persisted. Adjusted for errors and omissions, private investment fell by an additional $2^{1}/_{2}$ percentage points of GDP in 1992/93–1993/94. Part of the sluggishness of investment can be traced to the

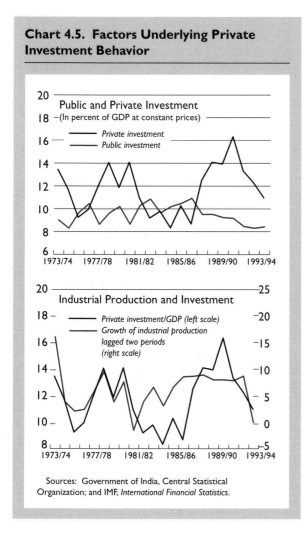

Chart 4.5. Factors Underlying Private Investment Behavior

Sources: Government of India, Central Statistical Organization; and IMF, *International Financial Statistics*.

lagged effects of the initial contraction in aggregate demand (see Table 4.4 and Chart 4.5, lower panel). Following steady annual growth of 8 percent from the mid-1980s onward, industrial production ground to a halt in 1991/92. The slowdown has been attributed to cutbacks in government orders and the process of industrial restructuring. The collapse of key export markets and the global recession of the early 1990s also played a role.

Price uncertainty—as proxied by the variance of inflation and of the real exchange rate—declined in 1992/93–1993/94. However, other sources of uncertainty may have contributed to the investment pause; the econometric results presented above predict a smaller decline in investment during this period than actually occurred. There may have been doubts about the sustainability of fiscal policy, which would affect not only macroeconomic variables such as inflation and interest rates but also the course of structural reform, especially public enterprise restructur-

ing or divestment, financial sector reform, and trade liberalization. Increased social and political tensions may also have contributed to heightened uncertainty.

The Investment Recovery of 1994/95–1995/96

The impact on private capital formation of the 1991 crisis—and the consequent stabilization and reform measures—was striking but brief. The evolution of key macroeconomic indicators in 1994/95 and early 1995/96 points to a strong export- and investment-led recovery. Most notable has been the rapid expansion of output in the capital goods sector, which was most adversely affected by the crisis. Capital goods production increased by more than 20 percent in 1994/95, notwithstanding a 60 percent decline in the average import-weighted tariff since 1990/91. Domestic borrowing also rose in 1994/95. The 10 percent increase in real credit to the private sector reflected a sharp rise in commercial bank borrowing and increased disbursements by the term lending institutions. The marked rise in capital goods imports and the steady increase in foreign direct investment are also indicative of a recovery in private capital formation.

The model forecasts a recovery of private capital formation to about $13^{1}/_{2}$ percent of GDP in 1994/95 from 11 percent in 1993/94, as a result of industrial recovery and easing of financial conditions. Investment is projected to rise further to almost 16 percent of GDP (the precrisis level) by 1995/96.

Appendix: Description of Variables

$$LIPE^{12} = \log \frac{\text{private investment/investment deflator}}{\text{GDP at market prices/GDP deflator}}$$

$$LIG^{13} = \log \frac{\text{public investment/investment deflator}}{\text{GDP at market prices/GDP deflator}}$$

$$RWGT = (1 + \text{weighted average lending rate})/(1 + \text{wholesale price index inflation}) - 1$$

$$RCRE^{14} = \frac{\frac{(\text{bcredit} + \text{termfin})/}{(\text{bcredit}(-1) + \text{termfin}(-1)))} - 1}{1 + \text{wholesale price index inflation (end-period)}}$$

$$LFRES = \log (\text{gross foreign reserves/months of merchandise imports})$$

---

[12]Includes private inventories and the errors and omissions term.

[13]Includes public inventories.

[14]"Bcredit" is the change in net banking system credit to the private sector. "Termfin" is the change in net credit from the term financing institutions to the private sector.

LSERVEX = log (external debt service/months of merchandise exports)

RGDP   = ((GDP/GDP(−1))/GDP deflator/GDP deflator(−1)) − 1

IIPGR   = (index of industrial production/index of industrial production(−1)) − 1

VINFL   = variance (monthly change in wholesale price index)

VREER   = variance (monthly change in real effective exchange rate)

VIIP   = variance (monthly change in index of industrial production (seasonally adjusted))

V   Fiscal Adjustment and Reform

Richard Hemming

The links between fiscal policy, investment, and growth are complex. Changes in the overall fiscal balance as well as in the structure of expenditure and taxation have important implications for investment and growth. This section examines the influences of each of these elements in turn over the recent reform period, before looking at the issue of center-state relations.

The Magnitude of Fiscal Adjustment

In 1990/91, the consolidated public sector deficit was $10^1/_2$ percent of GDP (Table 5.1). It had been high and rising throughout the second half of the 1980s. The upward trend was mainly the result of weakening central government finances, which in turn arose from an inelastic tax system and the rising burden of interest payments and other current expenditure. State government finances also deteriorated over this period, again because of stagnating revenues and rising current expenditure. Moreover, public enterprises were a drain on the budgets of both the central government and state governments.

In 1994/95, the public sector deficit still stood at $10^1/_2$ percent of GDP, but this unchanged position masked an uneven pattern of fiscal adjustment in the intervening period. In first two years of reform, the deficit fell by 2 percentage points of GDP. But this gain was more than lost in 1993/94 and then barely recovered in 1994/95.

The behavior of the public sector deficit over this period very much mirrored that of the central government deficit. Thus, the latter was reduced by about $2^1/_2$ percentage points of GDP between 1990/91 and 1992/93, mainly because of an increase in nontax revenue (including the proceeds from asset sales) and a reduction in capital expenditure (on infrastructure and loans to states and public enterprises). Central government public enterprises also contributed to fiscal adjustment, both through increased profits and lower capital spending. However, at the state level, despite an increase in tax collections over this period, higher spending led to a widening deficit.

To some extent, structural reforms led to the setback in 1993/94. Import duty reductions had a larger negative influence on revenue than was anticipated, while financial reforms raised interest costs.[1] There were also expenditure slippages, including a reversal of earlier cuts in defense spending. While state government finances showed little change, public enterprise investment picked up and contributed to a further increase in the overall deficit. In 1994/95, the beneficial impact of the strong expansion on revenue, as well as receipts from asset sales, contributed to a reduction in the central government deficit, but the financial position of the states is likely to have deteriorated further.[2]

Notwithstanding the subsequent slippage, the stabilization of the economy owed much to the initial fiscal adjustment, which increased the credibility of macroeconomic policy and bolstered business confidence. Nevertheless, the cutback in public sector investment of about 1 percent of GDP in 1991/92–1992/93 had an adverse multiplier effect through the economy and on certain sectors in particular (for example, capital goods) that contributed to the growth slowdown in this period. The relaxation of fiscal policy in 1993/94 helped to preserve a faltering growth momentum. But the legacy was a high deficit and increasing government indebtedness. This situation has raised serious questions about the medium-term sustainability of fiscal policy, as well as an immediate risk that public sector claims on private savings would crowd out private

---

[1]With stagnant imports and a reduction in the average (import-weighted) tariff from 64 percent to 47 percent, revenues from customs duties fell from 3.4 percent of GDP in 1992/93 to 2.8 percent of GDP in 1993/94. However, as discussed in Section VII, with the gradual elimination of tariff exemptions the collection rate fell only slightly from 32 percent in 1992/93 to 28 percent in 1993/94. Central government interest payments rose from 4.4 percent of GDP in 1992/93 to 4.7 percent of GDP in 1993/94; about half of this increase can be attributed to a rise in interest rates on government debt.

[2]Although revised estimates for the states' finances are not yet available for 1994/95, their deficit is estimated to have increased in part as a result of an unanticipated increase in resources received from small savings deposits. It is assumed that the states spent these additional resources.

Table 5.1. Fiscal Deficits
(In percent of GDP)

	1990/91	1991/92	1992/93	1993/94	Rev. Est. 1994/95
Public sector[1]	10.5	9.1	8.4	11.0	10.5
Central government	8.3	6.2	5.7	7.7	6.7
State governments	2.6	3.0	2.9	2.9	4.0
Public enterprises[2]	3.2	2.8	2.5	3.2	2.7

Sources: Government of India, budget documents and *Public Finance Statistics*; and IMF staff estimates.
[1]The public sector deficit is the sum of the deficits of the central government, state governments, and public enterprises less loans from the central government to state governments and public enterprises.
[2]Central government public enterprises only.

investment as the economic expansion gathered strength (Table 5.2).

Taxation

Tax revenue of central and state governments amounted to just over 16 percent of GDP in 1990/91, two thirds of which was collected by the central government. After the statutory sharing of personal income tax and excise duty revenue, the revenue shares were approximately equal.[3] The central government derived nearly 80 percent of its revenue from excise duties and customs duties, while the state governments collected 70 percent of their revenue from sales tax (Table 5.3). The emphasis on indirect taxation was, therefore, heavy. The tax ratio had increased by about 2 percentage points of GDP during the 1980s, with most of the increase from customs duties. This reflected the central government's tendency to raise discretionary revenue in a manner that would minimize the need to share the proceeds with state governments.

The pre-reform tax structure suffered from a number of structural deficiencies.

- Excise duties (the main domestic indirect tax) were levied by the central government on a narrow base, equivalent to about 20 percent of traded output in 1990/91. Agriculture and small-scale industry and commerce were the principal omissions. The structure of tax rates was also differentiated elaborately, with many specific rates. A rebate scheme for tax paid on inputs (MODVAT) had been introduced in 1986/87, but

[3]States received 85 percent of personal income tax revenue and 45 percent of excise duty revenue collected by the central government. These percentages were changed with effect from 1995/96 to 77.5 percent and 47.5 percent, respectively.

Table 5.2. Domestic Savings
(In percent of GDP)

	1990/91	1991/92	1992/93	1993/94	Rev. Est. 1994/95
Private savings	22.7	21.0	18.5	19.9	...
Public savings	1.0	2.1	1.5	0.2	...
Of which:					
Central government	−3.5	−2.7	−2.5	−4.4	−4.0
State governments	−0.2	−0.7	−0.5	...	...
Public sector claim on private savings	7.8	7.2	5.9	8.9	9.3

Sources: Government of India, *National Accounts Statistics*, budget documents, and *Public Finance Statistics*; and IMF staff estimates.

Table 5.3. Tax Revenue
(In percent of GDP)

	1990/91	1991/92	1992/93	1993/94	Rev. Est. 1994/95
Total tax revenue	16.2	16.7	16.3	15.3	15.8
Central taxes (gross)	10.8	10.9	10.6	9.6	9.9
Corporate tax	1.0	1.3	1.3	1.3	1.5
Personal tax	1.0	1.1	1.1	1.2	1.2
Excise taxes	4.6	4.6	4.4	4.0	4.1
Customs duties	3.9	3.6	3.4	2.8	2.9
Other	0.3	0.4	0.5	0.3	0.2
States' shares of central taxes	2.7	2.8	2.9	2.8	2.7
Central taxes (net)	8.0	8.1	7.7	6.8	7.2
State taxes	5.4	5.8	5.7	5.7	5.9
Sales tax	3.4	3.5	3.4	...	...
Memorandum items:					
Nontax revenue	2.7	3.5	3.7	3.4	3.9
Of which: Divestment proceeds[1]	—	0.4	0.3	—	0.6

Sources: Government of India, budget documents and *Public Finance Statistics*; and IMF staff estimates.
[1]Central government divestment proceeds only.

key sectors (including capital goods) were excluded. There was, therefore, significant cascading of tax rates, which together with the complex rate structure implied an arbitrary and distortionary tax structure.

- Customs duties were high and differentiated, with many general and user-specific exemptions. Because of high excise and customs duties on capital goods, effective protection was sometimes much less than the high customs duties alone would suggest. The pattern of effective protection was also highly variable, with little apparent economic rationale.
- Personal income tax had narrow coverage, with the tax base amounting to no more than 8 percent of GDP in 1990/91. Tax rates had been brought down and reduced in number during the 1980s, but the top rate of 50 percent, with a surcharge of 8 percent, was still high. For corporate tax, depreciation allowances and tax incentives were generous, offsetting high tax rates. The basic rates of 45 percent and 50 percent on domestic companies were also augmented by an 8 percent surcharge. The surcharges on the personal income tax and the corporate tax reached 12 percent and 15 percent, respectively.
- State sales taxes varied widely in coverage, point of collection, and rates. They were not integrated with excise duties, which compounded the distortionary impact of the latter.

- Tax administration was weak, resulting in high rates of noncompliance.

Since 1990/91, apart from an initial round of corporate tax and excise duty increases needed in support of stabilization, the central government has implemented a wide range of tax reforms aimed at producing a simpler and fairer tax system, consistent with fostering economic growth. These reforms have been guided by the report of the Chelliah Committee on tax reform (Tax Reforms Committee (1993)).

The principal feature of the tax reform has been the general lowering of tax rates (Table 5.4). Combined with a narrowing of the dispersion in tax rates, this has led to a reduction in distortions and disincentives. The structure of indirect taxes has also been improved. Most rates are now ad valorem, and many end-use exemptions have been eliminated. In addition, the MODVAT has been extended, most notably by the inclusion of the capital goods and petroleum sectors. A limited number of services (telephones, insurance (other than life insurance), and stockbrokers) are also taxed outside of the MODVAT. Import duties—particularly for capital goods, raw materials, and intermediate goods—have been lowered and restructured in tandem with trade liberalization. Rates are now converging to those recommended by the Chelliah Committee, with the average tariff rate now at 27 percent (incorporating

Table 5.4. Tax Rates
(In percent)

	1990/91	1994/95	Budget 1995/96
Excise duties			
Maximum rate	105	70	50
Import duties			
Average rate			
(import weighted)	87	33	27
Maximum rate	400	65	50
Personal income tax			
Maximum rate	54[1]	40	40
Corporate tax rate	49/54[1]	46[2]	46[2]

Sources: Indian authorities; World Bank; and IMF staff calculations.
[1]Includes 8 percent surcharge.
[2]Includes 15 percent surcharge.

Table 5.5. Central Government Revenue Shares
(In percent of gross tax revenue)

	1985/86	1990/91	1994/95
Income tax[1]	18.8	18.5	27.1
Excise duties	45.2	42.5	41.1
Import duties	33.2	35.8	29.5

Source: Government of India, budget documents.
[1]Corporate and personal tax.

the reductions in the 1995/96 budget), close to the Committee's target rate of 25 percent.

On the direct tax side, the personal exemption has been raised, the top rate has been lowered to 40 percent, and the surcharge has been withdrawn. Lower tax rates, administrative improvements, and increased use of tax withholding have raised the number of taxpayers. The corporate tax is now levied at a uniform rate of 40 percent on domestic companies, but the 15 percent surcharge has been retained. To improve tax administration, there has been increasing use of minimum taxes and withholding, and computerization is being introduced. However, progress with reducing exemptions for both personal and corporate tax has been slow.

The recent reforms have produced a significant shift in the structure of tax revenue from trade taxes to income taxes, as shown in Table 5.5. This shift should allow redistributional objectives to be addressed more fully and systematically, which will be an important element in ensuring that growth is sustainable. In addition, lower import duties will make Indian industry more competitive, while reduced taxes on capital and intermediate goods will lessen distortions in production and encourage investment. Nevertheless, the tax-to-GDP ratio remains lower than in 1990/91, and greater effort is needed to increase the tax base. Widening the bases of the personal income tax and the corporate tax, by reducing exemptions and other tax concessions, is especially important and would provide the basis for further rate cuts and the elimination of the surcharges.

The final steps to move to a more comprehensive value-added tax (VAT) at the central level will gen-

erate dynamic efficiency gains over time, even if the short-term revenue benefits will be small. There is immediate scope to impose indirect taxation on a wider range of services, either inside or outside the VAT. But perhaps the greatest remaining task is to replace the sales tax at the state level with a VAT, which would allow the elimination of important distortions (including the taxing of interstate trade), as well as more effective taxation of wholesale and retail margins.

Expenditure

Data shortcomings complicate the analysis of public expenditure trends in India and their impact on investment and growth. Indian public finance data distinguish between current and capital expenditure, development and nondevelopment expenditure, and plan and nonplan expenditure. None of these clearly separates public consumption from public investment or, more generally, productive from unproductive expenditure. A breakdown of expenditure into economically meaningful categories provides some guidance, but in India such a breakdown is only available for central government expenditure, which is half of the total, and available only with a considerable lag.[4] Moreover, the states are responsible for most expenditure on infrastructure and social programs, on which only limited information is available.

Central government current expenditure at the beginning of the reform period was dominated by interest payments, defense spending, subsidies, and grants to states (Table 5.6). Much of the noninterest expenditure was unproductive. For example, the subsidy program for fertilizers not only had a high budgetary cost but also introduced a serious price

---

[4]The data are adjusted for transfers from the central government to states.

Table 5.6. Central Government Expenditure
(In percent of GDP)

	1990/91	1991/92	1992/93	1993/94	Rev. Est. 1994/95
Total expenditure	19.1	17.8	17.0	17.8	17.7
Current expenditure	15.1	14.8	14.5	15.3	14.9
Interest	4.0	4.3	4.4	4.7	4.8
Major subsidies	1.3	1.4	1.2	1.3	1.2
Defense[1]	2.9	2.7	2.5	2.8	2.6
Grants to states	2.5	2.6	2.6	2.7	2.3
Wages	2.0	1.9	1.8	1.9	1.7
Other	2.4	1.9	1.9	1.9	2.3
Capital expenditure	4.0	3.0	2.5	2.5	2.8
Economic services	1.3	0.9	0.9	0.7	0.7
Of which: Infrastructure	1.0	0.7	0.6	0.6	...
Loans to states (net)	1.8	1.5	1.3	1.2	1.5
Other	0.9	0.6	0.3	0.6	0.6

Sources: Government of India, budget documents and *Public Finance Statistics*.
[1]Includes defense capital expenditure.

distortion. Despite efforts to contain spending, with rising interest payments and subsidies current expenditure increased throughout the 1980s, and resources were drawn from capital programs, including loans to states and infrastructure, as well as operations and maintenance.

State current expenditure also rose, particularly the wage bill (Table 5.7). Consequently, infrastructure investment was squeezed, while other programs controlled by the states—most notably education, health, and poverty alleviation programs—did not receive sufficient funding. At the same time, rates of return on projects were low, partly because little use was made of proper investment appraisal techniques and poor management of programs. Many social programs were inefficient. Health and education programs paid insufficient attention to basic education and health care, while the increasing share of spending taken up by wages led to shortages of teaching materials and medical equipment. Anti-poverty programs did not always reach the intended beneficiaries. In particular, the large, high-profile programs that pre-empted most resources—the Integrated Rural Development Program, the Public Distribution System, and the main rural public works program—were subject to significant leakages and high administrative overheads.

The pattern of expenditure adjustment for the 1990/91–1994/95 reform period is shown in Table 5.8, which reports the elasticity of individual expenditure components with respect to total expenditure.

Current expenditure has risen twice as fast as total expenditure, although much of this reflects rising interest payments. The elasticity of noninterest current expenditures has been substantially less than 1, with the negative elasticities for both subsidies and wages

Table 5.7. State Government Expenditure
(In percent of GDP)

	1990/91	1991/92	1992/93	1993/94	1994/95
Total expenditure	14.2	16.3	15.9	16.1	16.7
Current expenditure	11.8	14.0	13.6	...	...
Capital expenditure	2.4	2.3	2.3	...	...

Source: Government of India, *Public Finance Statistics*.

Table 5.8. Central Government Expenditure Elasticities, 1990/91–1994/95

	Change in Real Expenditure	Elasticity with Respect to Total Expenditure
Total expenditure	6.4	. . .
Current expenditure	13.1	2.0
Interest	38.8	6.0
Noninterest	3.8	0.6
Subsidies	−23.4	−3.6
Defense	3.5	0.5
Grants to states	5.3	0.8
Wages	−1.8	−0.3
Other	33.1	5.3
Capital expenditure	−18.8	−2.9
Economic services	−31.2	−4.9
Loans to states	10.3	1.6

Sources: Indian authorities; and IMF staff calculations.

showing that these—and especially the former—have borne a significant share of expenditure adjustment. In the case of subsidies, the negative elasticity in large part reflects the elimination of export subsidies. Capital expenditure as a whole has an elasticity of almost −3, with the elasticity for spending on economic services (which includes infrastructure) being especially negative.

Expenditure reform has clearly lagged behind tax reform. The composition of spending is still skewed toward unproductive expenditures. The reduction in the wage bill has reflected more a squeeze on real wage rates than reductions in excess labor. Inefficient food and fertilizer subsidy programs remain in place. Although allocations for social sectors and poverty programs have generally been protected, albeit at low levels, little action has been taken to improve program efficiency.[5] A thorough reappraisal of the structure of expenditure is called for, supported by more effective expenditure control mechanisms. Greater emphasis needs to be placed on maintenance spending; reducing excess labor; reordering expenditure priorities; improved program design, management, and implementation, thus curbing leakages and administrative overheads; cost recovery (especially for higher education and curative health care); and an expanded role for the private sector.

Center-State Relations

The fiscal adjustment process since 1990/91 has relied heavily on measures taken by the central government, which indicates the constraints that the federal system of government places on the center's ability to influence state finances. The constitution assigns to the states primary responsibility in a number of key expenditure areas and the right to levy certain taxes. States then receive formula-based shares of central tax revenue, as well as grants and loans. While in principle grants and loans have a discretionary element, in practice this has been limited. The central government has therefore restricted states' ability to borrow and has raised the cost of borrowing to market levels to impose financial discipline upon them. But this has not provided sufficient leverage to force states to address their four major problems: a weak revenue effort; a growing wage bill; uneconomic enterprises (especially in the areas of electricity distribution and transportation); and low cost recovery.

State finances need to be strengthened, for both macroeconomic and structural reasons. As regards the former, the risk is that expansionary policies on the part of states will compromise fiscal adjustment at the center. From the latter standpoint, the inefficiency of state spending programs curtails the scope for efficiency gains from adjustment by the center. In particular, inadequate infrastructure and human capital—both of which are substantially state responsibilities—have large spillover costs. Similarly, inefficient state taxes can limit the benefits from the reform of central taxes.

Shifting the burden of adjustment to the states requires a change in the way expenditure decisions are made by states. In particular, their discretionary spending should be limited by their ability to raise the revenue to pay for it. This in turn requires that states be provided with a flexible, nondistortionary source of own revenue. In this connection, introduction of a state-level VAT, as a supplement to an expanded central MODVAT, would be an important measure. This has to be accompanied by revenue-sharing and transfer arrangements that impose expenditure discipline by not validating discretionary spending. In particular, the total resources flowing from the center to the states—revenue shares, grants, and loans—should be guided by the expenditure responsibilities assigned to them rather than the spending they choose to undertake.[6] In combination with tight

---

[5]For example, a large part of the expenditure under the "public distribution system" is due to the high costs of the Food Corporation of India, including its excessive staffing and inefficiencies in its purchase, storage, and transport operations.

[6]The Tenth Finance Commission (Ministry of Finance (1994)) has recommended that grants-in-aid, which at present are set to fill anticipated resource shortfalls at the state level, be phased out. In addition, the Commission has recommended that a uniform rate be applied across all taxes collected by the center in determining the states' share of these taxes.

Table 5.9. Fiscal Operations
(In percent of GDP)

	1990/91	1991/92	1992/93	1993/94	Rev. Est. 1994/95
Consolidated public sector[1]					
Revenue and grants	20.7	23.0	23.0	21.7	22.8
Expenditure and net lending	31.2	32.0	31.4	32.7	33.2
Interest payments	5.2	6.1	6.4	6.7	6.7
Primary deficit	−5.3	−3.0	−2.0	−4.3	−3.8
Overall public sector deficit	−10.5	−9.1	−8.4	−11.0	−10.5
(Net of asset sales)	−10.5	−9.6	−8.7	−11.0	−11.1
Public sector debt	77.0	83.1	85.4	90.1	88.6
Memorandum items:					
Central government deficit	−8.6	−6.3	−5.7	−7.7	−6.7
States' deficit[2]	−2.6	−3.0	−2.9	−2.9	−4.0
Central public enterprises' deficit	−3.2	−2.8	−2.5	−3.2	−2.7

Sources: Data provided by the Indian authorities; and IMF staff estimates.

[1]The consolidated public sector comprises the operations of the central government, the state governments, and the central public enterprises.

[2]The figures for the states' deficit in 1994/95 are IMF staff estimates.

control of borrowing, this would impose a hard budget constraint on states, which would in turn force them to control wages, to improve enterprise efficiency, and to increase cost recovery.

The Need for Fiscal Consolidation

A central policy challenge facing India is to reduce its extremely high public sector deficit. Continuing high deficits have a number of adverse consequences:

- The task of preserving macroeconomic stability is complicated as a heavy burden is put on monetary policy.
- There is a risk of a rising public debt and debt-service burden that would eventually become unsustainable.
- National savings are lowered, thus reducing the scope for domestic investment without heavy reliance on foreign savings.
- The pace of structural reform could be slowed, particularly trade liberalization and financial sector reform.

As noted earlier in this section, the stabilization of the economy owed much to the initial reduction in the central government fiscal deficit. However, in view of the subsequent fiscal slippage at the central level and a deterioration of the states' fiscal position, the consolidated public sector deficit in 1994/95 remained around its level in 1990/91 (Table 5.9).

Thus, the stock of public sector debt is estimated to have reached about 90 percent of GDP, which is very high by international comparison.[7] Also of concern is the high primary deficit of the consolidated public sector, estimated to be nearly 4 percent of GDP in 1994/95.

Until recently, India financed its deficits to a large extent by borrowing domestically (including from the central bank) at below-market interest rates. The maintenance of high cash reserve and statutory liquidity ratios on bank deposits created a captive market for low-interest government debt. Four years ago, over two thirds of bank deposits were pre-empted by the government because of these high ratios, thereby eroding bank profitability. However, a number of steps have been taken since 1991 to strengthen the financial system and to shift government borrowing to market terms. This has contributed to a rise of about 2 percentage points in the implicit interest rate on outstanding government debt to about 10 percent.[8] The shift to market borrowing in the context of high primary deficits has meant a sharp increase in the government's interest bill, which has risen from 5¼ percent of GDP in 1990/91 to almost 7 percent of GDP in 1994/95 (see

---

[7]This figure represents the gross liabilities of the consolidated public sector, which comprises the operations of the central government, the state governments, and the central public enterprises, but not the state public enterprises.

[8]The marginal cost of government borrowing, for example through a ten-year bond, is about 14 percent at present.

Table 5.9). Interest payments absorb nearly one third of public sector revenue, and over one fourth of current spending.

India's high fiscal deficit has created tensions in macroeconomic management and hindered progress in structural reform. The trade-offs between the authorities' multiple objectives of containing the debt-service burden, reforming the financial system, controlling inflation, and achieving rapid growth have become increasingly evident. The tightening of liquidity since October 1994 has contributed to rising real interest rates, a reduction in banks' holdings of excess government securities, and increased difficulties in managing the borrowing program. Given the rising cost of borrowing in the market, there are increasing pressures on the Reserve Bank to accommodate the fiscal deficit. The high deficit also hinders the progress in financial sector reform; limited flexibility in fiscal policy has encouraged the use of directed credit programs to achieve development objectives, while the cash reserve requirement and the statutory liquidity ratio remain high. Furthermore, continued import tariff reductions may be affected by concerns about the potential loss of revenue from a reduction in rates.

Sustainable fiscal consolidation will require vigorous efforts by all levels of the public sector—the center, states, and public enterprises. In this connection, although a restructuring and streamlining of expenditures is required, it is unlikely that the overall ratio of government spending relative to GDP can be brought down appreciably. Interest payments will continue to rise, while the heavy demands for productive spending in areas such as infrastructure, education, and health care would need to be met. Inevitably, therefore, much of the deficit reduction would need to be achieved by raising the ratio of revenues to GDP. This will require continuing efforts to broaden the tax base so that revenue yield can be increased without adversely affecting economic efficiency.

As discussed above, the states will need to make a greater contribution to the adjustment process. Accelerated public enterprise reform could also contribute to fiscal adjustment. Improved profitability of public enterprises would boost dividend payments and reduce the need for direct budget support, without jeopardizing essential public investments. An ambitious divestment program could generate resources to retire domestic debt, thus lowering interest costs.

In conclusion, without substantial fiscal adjustment, it will be difficult to achieve both low inflation and the rapid growth that is needed to make effective inroads against poverty. Although the task will not be easy, with determined efforts it should be feasible to eliminate the primary deficit of the consolidated public sector by the end of this decade.

VI Recent Experience with a Surge in Capital Inflows

Charles Collyns

A striking aspect of India's recent experience has been a remarkable surge in foreign investment. Historically, private capital flows to India have been low, discouraged by a tight regulatory regime as well as a highly distorted economy. However, with a liberalization of controls on capital inflows as well as the broader impact of reforms on India's economic prospects, India has attracted substantial foreign investor interest during 1993/94 and 1994/95. Over this period, India accounted for a larger volume of international equity issues than any other emerging market. Share purchases on local exchanges have also been heavy, while foreign direct investment has increased appreciably. Taken together, these inflows were a major contributor to the recent strengthening of India's external position and added substantially to the resources available for investment. However, as in other countries, the surge in inflows complicated the task of macroeconomic management by making monetary control more difficult and putting upward pressure on inflation.

This section reviews the recent experience with capital inflows and assesses their impact on the Indian economy. It first looks at the pattern of recent flows, contrasts India's experience with that of other countries that have also recently received large private inflows, and considers the factors underlying the flows. Next, it examines the impact of resource flows on firms, on the macroeconomic environment, and on the financial system. Finally, the sustainability of capital inflows to India is assessed in the wake of the Mexican crisis.

Recent Experience

Overall Trends

Prior to 1991, capital flows to India predominantly consisted of aid flows, commercial borrowing, and nonresident Indian (NRI) deposits (Table 6.1). Direct investment was limited, averaging around $200 million a year over 1985–91. Foreign companies wishing to invest in India were generally restricted to 40 percent equity participation, sub-

jected to requirements on technology transfer, and limited to priority areas. Foreign portfolio investment was channeled almost exclusively into a limited number of public sector bond issues, while foreign equity holdings in Indian companies were not permitted.

A key component of the economic reform program launched in July 1991 has been the adoption of a much more open approach to foreign investment. At the outset, approval for direct investment participation up to 51 percent in priority areas was made automatic, while the criteria for approval were liberalized more generally. In February 1992, it was announced that Indian firms in good standing would be allowed to raise funds through equity and convertible bond issues in Euromarkets, and in September 1992, registered foreign institutional investors (FIIs) were allowed to purchase both equity and debt securities directly on local markets.[1] A single FII may hold up to 5 percent of a company's issued share capital, while all FIIs together may hold up to 24 percent of a company's capital. To encourage these flows further, in the March 1993 budget the tax on interest and dividend income on FII holdings was set at 20 percent, while capital gains tax was set at 30 percent on investments held for less than one year and 10 percent thereafter.[2] After an initial delay, the response to these liberalization measures was strong. Total foreign direct and portfolio investment rose to $5.1 billion in 1993/94, from $585 million in 1992/93 and $148 million in 1991/92 (Table 6.2). Inflows continued at a high rate through November 1994 and, although there was a slowdown in portfolio inflows in the final months of the year, the total for the year still reached $4.8 billion.

Most dramatic was the surge in Euroissues. In 1992/93, there were two global depository receipt

---

[1]In view of concerns about external indebtedness, FIIs may not hold more than 30 percent of their portfolios in debt instruments. Initially, the 30 percent rule applied to each individual fund administered by an FII. This restriction was relaxed in December 1993 to be applied to each FII's portfolio as a whole.

[2]Capital gains tax is avoided altogether by investment funds registered in Mauritius, which sets no capital gains tax and has a double taxation treaty with India.

Table 6.1. Capital Account
(In millions of U.S. dollars)

	(Annual Average) 1985/86–1990/91	1991/92	1992/93	1993/94	Est. 1994/95
Capital account	7,347	3,420	2,785	8,506	7,767
Direct and portfolio investment[1]	209	154	585	5,104	4,799
Net aid	2,525	2,489	1,454	1,344	1,533
Net commercial borrowing	1,945	1,456	−358	−155	−118
Nonresident deposits	1,917	290	2,001	940	1,000
Other	753	−969	−897	1,273	552
Memorandum items:					
Current account	−7,469	−1,638	−3,888	−685	−1,388
(In percent of GDP)	...	−0.7	−1.6	−0.3	−0.5
Overall balance	−122	1,782	−1,103	7,821	6,379
Change in gross international reserves (increase +)	−606	3,521	1,041	8,815	5,773

Sources: Ministry of Finance; and IMF staff estimates.

[1] Foreign currency convertible bonds and floating rate notes are included in direct and portfolio investment.

(GDR) issues totaling $241 million, as the initial interest of foreign investors was dampened by the stock market scam in May 1992, as well as by related concerns about market practices and the collapse in stock prices (Chart 6.1). By contrast, in 1993/94 17 GDR issues raised $1.5 billion, and 10 foreign currency convertible bond (FCCB) issues raised a total of $1 billion (Tables 6.3 and 6.4).

The bulk of issues occurred in early 1994 as the stock market recovered. Foreign investor enthusiasm rose to such a height that new GDRs could be issued at a premium to prices on local markets (Chart 6.2).

Issuance continued to be heavy for the first eight months of 1994/95. A further 25 GDR issues raised $1.8 billion, while two floating rate note (FRN) is-

Table 6.2. Foreign Direct and Portfolio Investment
(In millions of U.S. dollars)

	1990/91	1991/92	1992/93	1993/94	Est. 1994/95
Total	165	148	585	5,104	4,799
Foreign direct investment	165	148	344	620	1,000
Automatic approval by Reserve Bank	—	—	43	89	...
SIA/FIPB approvals	...	85	240	314	...
NRI schemes	...	62	61	217	...
Foreign portfolio investment	—	—	242	4,484	3,799
Equity	—	—	242	3,490	3,464
FII	—	—	1	1,700	1,419
GDRs	—	—	241	1,460	2,045
NRI	—	—	—	10	...
Offshore funds	—	—	—	320	...
Equity related	—	—	—	994	35
FCCBs	—	—	—	994	35
Bonds	—	—	—	—	300
FRNs	—	—	—	—	300

Source: Ministry of Finance.

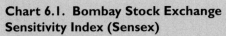

Chart 6.1. Bombay Stock Exchange Sensitivity Index (Sensex)

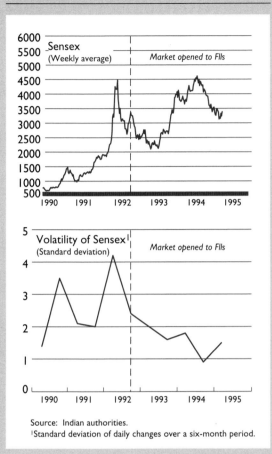

Source: Indian authorities.
[1]Standard deviation of daily changes over a six-month period.

sues raised $300 million. However, issues have slowed sharply since December 1994, against the background of generally unsettled conditions in international financial markets. Even before the Mexican crisis in mid-December, demand for Indian GDRs had weakened, and new GDRs were issued at significant discounts relative to prices of the underlying stocks on local exchanges. Moreover, there were signs of market saturation, and a number of issues were delayed or canceled. The pace of issuance was also affected by guidelines established by the Ministry of Finance, which was concerned at the liquidity effects of the capital inflows. From May 1994, issues were subject to restrictions on the end-use of funds, and new approvals for FCCB issues were limited to cases involving a restructuring of existing external debt. The guidelines were further modified in October 1994 to require that funds raised be held overseas until utilized for authorized investments.

Like Euroissues, direct share purchases by FIIs on local exchanges were initially slow but burgeoned in late 1993 to such an extent that existing custodial capacity became saturated and share transfer procedures needed to be streamlined.[3] Net inflows through this route amounted to $1.7 billion in 1993/94 as a whole, with a further $320 million of FII funds being deposited in offshore accounts prior to investment in local markets (Table 6.5). Net inflows continued at an average of $175 million a month through October 1994, before tapering off in the last five months of the fiscal year. It is noteworthy that net inflows remained positive throughout the year, although there was some increase in sales by FIIs in the immediate wake of the Mexican crisis. By the end of March 1995, a cumulative total of over $3 billion had been invested in Indian equity by FIIs. By contrast, to date there has been virtually no investment in local debt instruments.

Direct investment inflows have also built up, albeit more slowly, rising to $344 million in 1992/93, $620 million in 1993/94, and an estimated $1 billion in 1994/95. The bulk of the investment has been in joint ventures; only about 10 percent of approvals have been for 100 percent foreign ownership. About one fourth of this inflow occurred through special share issues to foreign partners seeking to raise their stake in existing ventures. Actual flows are still small relative to approved investments: proposals amounting to about $6 billion were approved from August 1991 to March 1995, 85 percent of which were in priority sectors. Reflecting the more liberal framework, the Foreign Investment Promotion Board's rejection rate fell from 40–50 percent prior to 1991 to under 10 percent in 1993, while about 30 percent of approvals have been through the automatic route.

Investor Base

To date, the investor base for portfolio flows to India has been relatively narrow. The bulk of funding has come from regional and country funds aimed primarily at individual equity investors. During 1993/94, 11 India-dedicated country funds were launched, raising a total of $2.7 billion. Market participants suggest that these funds were targeted mainly at U.S. and U.K. individual investors, although a portion of the resources—perhaps around one fourth—is believed to have been contributed by nonresident Indians or returning "hawala" money (that is, flight capital). Interest from other Asian investors has been mainly from Hong Kong; Japanese portfolio investment has been limited in part because

[3]These included the introduction of jumbo transfer certificates and simplification of procedures for application of stamp tax.

Table 6.3. Indian GDR Issues

Year/ Month	Name of Company	Sector	Industrial Grouping	Net Sales Rank[1]	Issue Size (In millions of U.S. dollars)	Market Capitalization[2] (In billions of rupees)	Ratio of Issue Size to Market Capitalization (In percent)	GDR Premium over Domestic Price at Issue (In percent)	Current GDR Premium Relative to Domestic Price at Issue[3] (In percent)	Current GDR Premium Relative to Current Domestic Price[3] (In percent)
1992/93										
May	RIL	Diversified	Reliance	1	150.4	61.6	7.4	-13.7	-1.7	8.4
Nov.	Grasim	Diversified	Birla	7	90.1	32.7	8.3	-17.1	55.4	31.3
Total					240.5					
1993/94										
July	Hindalco	Aluminum	Birla	19	72.0	25.6	8.8	-48.5	—	9.7
Sept.	SPIC	Fertilizers	—	10	74.8	5.6	42.2	-22.3	-21.6	22.9
Oct.	Bombay Dyeing	Textiles	—	42	50.0	10.4	15.1	-2.6	21.6	-6.2
Oct.	ITC	Diversified	ITC	4	68.9	61.0	3.5	-9.2	3.6	-3.6
Nov.	Mahindra and Mahindra	Automobiles	—	9	74.8	4.4	53.0	-12.6	29.0	9.7
Jan.	Great Eastern Shipping	Shipping	—	79	100.0	13.4	23.4	14.3	-39.1	5.7
Jan.	Indian Rayon	Diversified	Birla	25	125.0	9.3	42.0	10.8	-16.3	13.6
Jan.	Indo-Gulf Fertilizers	Fertilizers	Birla	58	100.0	9.0	34.9	107.6	17.5	12.0
Jan.	Videocon International	Electricals	Videocon	26	90.0	6.7	42.0	6.4	-52.0	10.5
Feb.	Arvind Mills	Textiles	Labhai	98	125.0	6.9	56.4	10.6	-50.5	1.9
Feb.	Indian Aluminium	Aluminum	—	32	60.0	9.6	19.7	7.9	11.7	6.1
Feb.	Jain Irrigation	Miscellaneous	—	...	30.0	...	...	12.5	-48.9	-0.1
Feb.	RIL	Diversified	Reliance	1	300.0	61.6	15.3	-3.9	-25.7	6.4
Feb.	Tata Electrical	Power	Tata	18	75.0	7.6	30.9	4.8	-34.3	27.7
Feb.	United Phosphorus	Pesticides	—	204	55.0	4.2	41.3	-3.7	-39.5	5.0
Feb.	Wockhardt	Drugs	...	...	75.0	...	...	135.3	-28.2	-6.0
Mar.	Garden Silk Mills	Textiles	...	105	45.0	1.7	80.5	-5.1	-72.0	-22.1
Total					1,520.5					
1994/95										
Apr.	Calcutta Electricity	Power	—	23	125.0	4.0	98.8	-1.6	-49.3	-14.7
May	DCW	Chemicals	—	191	25.0	2.2	36.2	-15.0	-13.7	10.7
May	Tube Investments	Transport	—	80	45.0	1.4	100.8	-12.8	-40.2	7.7
May	Grasim	Diversified	Birla	7	100.0	32.3	9.6	-5.4	13.0	31.3
June	Core Parenteral	Pharmaceuticals	...	...	70.0	...	...	-8.1	-52.6	-9.3
July	Ranbaxy Labs	Pharmaceuticals	—	45	100.0	8.3	37.9	-11.6	13.0	21.5
July	Telco	Automobiles	Tata	3	100.0	42.8	7.3	-7.1	31.1	25.0
July	Hindalco	Aluminum	Birla	19	100.0	25.6	12.3	-19.9	4.3	9.7
July	Finolex Cable	Cables	—	156	100.0	3.2	96.4	-16.7	-36.0	1.1
July	EID Parry	Diversified	—	82	40.0	1.4	89.6	-15.1	-57.0	-19.1
July	Dr. Reddy's	Pharmaceuticals	—	275	48.0	2.3	64.0	-30.0	-31.7	0.5
Aug.	Sanghi Polyester	Textiles	—	270	50.0	2.9	53.4	-25.0	-51.0	-10.5
Aug.	S.I. Viscose	Textiles	—	111	45.0	3.4	41.4	-0.1	-23.5	-1.1
Aug.	JCT Ltd.	Textiles	Thapar	78	45.0	5.3	26.7	-29.1	-27.8	-5.8
Sept.	Century Textiles	Textiles	—	11	100.0	29.7	10.6	-10.0	-39.7	-6.3

Oct.	E.I. Hotels	Hotels	Oberoi	207	100.0	5.7	22.1	-6.7	-54.0	-12.8
Oct.	Gujarat Narmada	Fertilizers	Gujarat public sector undertaking	35	55.0	8.6	20.1	-4.9	15.9	31.8
Oct.	India Cements	Cement	—	60	45.0	3.9	36.6	-15.8	-39.7	1.5
Oct.	Usha Beltron	Cables	—	...	35.0	...	...	-24.8	-12.1	9.9
Oct.	J.K. Corp.	Diversified	Singhania	36	55.0	18.2	...	-8.0	-44.1	-2.8
Oct.	Shriram Ind. Ent.	Diversified	Shriram	12	40.0	12.0	6.9	-22.9	-42.1	-3.4
Oct.	Bajaj Auto	Automobiles	Bajaj	6	110.0	43.0	28.9	1.9	16.1	24.3
Nov.	L & T	Machinery	—	...	150.0	...	10.7	-10.8	1.5	10.0
Nov.	NEPC Micon	Diversified	—	...	48.0	...	...	-24.7	-46.7	0.2
Nov.	Raymond Wool	Diversified	Singhania	35	60.0	9.7	19.5	-18.1	-25.4	-6.1
Dec.	IPCL	Petrochemicals	Central public sector undertaking							
Mar.	Ashok Leyland	Automobiles	—	16	100.0	9.5	45.9	-10.7	14.2	10.1
Total					137.8					
					2,028.8					

Sources: Ministry of Finance; and press reports.

[1] Pertains to sales in 1992/93.

[2] As of March 31, 1993.

[3] As of April 21, 1995.

Table 6.4. Eurobond Issues by Indian Companies

Year/ Month	Company's Name	Sector	Type	Industrial Grouping	Interest Rate[1]	Tenor (In years)	Currency Denomination	Amount (In millions of U.S. dollars)
1993/94								
July	Essar Gujarat	Sponge iron	FCCB	—	5.50	5.00	US$	75.0
Oct.	Jindal Strips	Steel	FCCB	Jindal	4.25	5.25	US$	60.5
Oct.	RIL	Diversified	FCCB	Reliance	3.50	6.00	US$	140.0
Oct.	SCICI	Financial	FCCB	—	3.50	10.50	US$	100.0
Nov.	Gujarat Ambuja Cement	Cement	FCCB	—	3.50	5.50	US$	80.0
Dec.	Sterlite Industries	Cables	FCCB	Khaitan	3.50	5.50	US$	100.0
Jan.	Bharat Forge	Forging	FCCB	—			SF	14.0
Feb.	ICICI	Financial	FCCB	—	2.50	6.00	US$	200.0
Feb.	Nippon Denro Ispat	Steel	FCCB	—	3.00	7.00	US$	125.0
Feb.	Tisco	Steel	FCCB	Tata	2.25	6.00	US$	100.0
Total								994.5
1994/95								
May	Ballarpur Industries	Diversified	FCCB	—	4.00	5.00	US$	35.0
July	IDBI	Financial	FRN	—	LIBOR + 110	5.00	US$	100.0
Aug.	Essar Gujarat	Sponge iron	FRN	—	LIBOR + 265	5.00	US$	200.0
Total								335.0

Sources: Ministry of Finance; and press reports.

[1]Coupon rates for FCCBs.

Indian stock exchanges have not yet been approved by the Japanese Ministry of Finance.[4] Some of the FII inflows have come from hedge funds, which take an aggressive approach to portfolio management. Interest to date from pension funds and other institutional investors has apparently been limited.[5]

About one third of approved direct investment has involved U.S. companies. Other important investors include European Union countries, Japan, Switzerland, and nonresident Indians.

Comparison with Other Countries

India's recent experience with portfolio inflows has been part of a broader phenomenon of increasing access by developing countries to private capital. Indeed, in comparison with a number of other countries in East Asia and Latin America, if not to its own past, the scale of total flows to India has remained modest (Table 6.6). Nonetheless, foreign investment

flows to India have been substantially larger than those to neighbors in South Asia, even taking into account the smaller size of their economies.

The concentration in equity portfolio flows rather than in debt or direct investment has been a major

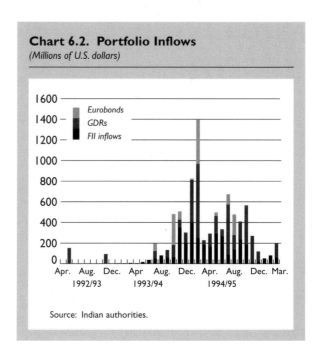

Chart 6.2. Portfolio Inflows
(Millions of U.S. dollars)

Source: Indian authorities.

---

[4]Japanese-based securities houses can only undertake transactions on approved exchanges on behalf of their clients. Lack of transparency and problems with trading rules have been cited as reasons for noninclusion of Indian exchanges in the list of approved foreign stock exchanges issued by the Japanese Ministry of Finance.

[5]See Goldstein and Folkerts-Landau (1994) for more general background on the investor base for recent private flows to developing countries.

Table 6.5. Investments by Foreign Institutional Investors
(In millions of U.S. dollars)

Year/Month	Purchases	Sales	Net
1992/93			
Jan.	0.2	—	0.2
Feb.	0.4	—	0.4
Mar.	5.0	1.3	3.7
Total	5.6	1.3	4.3
1993/94			
Apr.	1.6	0.1	1.5
May	13.4	0.1	13.3
June	33.7	0.2	33.5
July	46.3	0.7	45.6
Aug.	81.0	4.6	76.4
Sept.	57.4	1.2	56.2
Oct.	61.0	2.4	58.6
Nov.	351.4	3.2	348.2
Dec.	207.2	7.8	199.4
Jan.	411.7	18.1	393.6
Feb.	291.9	46.5	245.4
Mar.	245.9	65.6	180.3
Total	1,802.5	150.5	1,652.0
1994/95			
Apr.	229.1	64.1	165.0
May	335.8	46.8	289.0
June	349.6	88.2	261.4
July	137.0	55.0	82.0
Aug.	195.4	61.5	133.9
Sept.	293.2	62.8	230.4
Oct.	269.0	86.1	182.9
Nov.	98.1	88.0	10.1
Dec.	118.6	103.1	15.5
Jan.	155.4	106.9	48.5
Feb.	129.7	65.0	64.7
Mar.	127.2	72.0	55.2
Total	2,438.1	899.5	1,547.2

Sources: Securities Exchange Board of India; Ministry of Finance; and press reports.

securities and bonds issued by public sector undertakings) have tended to be illiquid, particularly since the discovery of trading malpractices in public sector bonds at the time of the stock market scam.

Regarding direct investment, actual flows relative to GDP in India remain much smaller than in the successful East Asian countries and a number of Latin American countries, in large part because the reforms were launched much later in India than in these countries. The realization of projects has also been slowed by the need to establish appropriate policy frameworks for sectors—like hydrocarbons, power, and telecommunications—only recently opened for private participation. In addition, a number of institutional concerns remain entrenched that have dampened investor interest, including bureaucratic procedures, inflexible labor policies, and a slow-moving legal system (Bhattacharya (1994)).

The Indian experience has also differed from that of other countries in the degree to which foreign investment has been concentrated in the private rather than the public sector. Again, the contrast is particularly sharp with Latin American countries where the re-entry into capital markets was spearheaded by sovereign bond issues and foreign investments connected with privatization. In India, foreign investment into the public sector has been largely limited to FII purchases of shares disinvested by the government. To date, only two public sector companies have issued GDRs, both at the tail end of the surge in issuance, probably because of their lack of autonomy in decision making, which restricts their flexibility in approaching the market. For instance, a jumbo issue by the state telephone company (Videsh Sanchar Nigam Ltd.) was withdrawn from the market in May 1994 after it became apparent that the issue could not be completed at the originally anticipated price.

Factors Behind the Flows

Both external and internal factors accounted for the global surge in private capital flows to developing countries.[6] India was no exception to this pattern. The external factors were both cyclical and structural. On the cyclical side, the slow and uneven recovery in industrial countries in 1992 and 1993 implied a depressed global demand for capital and low anticipated rates of return for most assets. Structural changes in international financial markets that encouraged flows to developing countries include the growing importance of professional investment managers in allocating savings, the increasingly global availability of information, and the introduction of instruments to hedge

difference between the Indian experience and that of other recipient countries. In Latin American countries in particular, international bond issues and investments in local currency debt instruments (including bank deposits, certificates of deposit, and treasury bills) have accounted for a large share of the total. In India, by contrast, the Ministry of Finance has kept a tight check on international debt issues (including convertible bonds) as a means to control overall indebtedness, while foreign use of bank accounts in India has remained restricted to transaction purposes. Another factor discouraging foreign interest in local debt instruments has been that secondary markets for such instruments (such as government

---

[6]See, for example, the discussion in International Monetary Fund (1994), Chapter IV, and in Dunaway and others (1995).

Table 6.6. Direct and Portfolio Investment in Selected Developing Countries, 1993–94

	Net Direct Investment	Net Portfolio Investment	Total	Total Relative to			
				GDP	Exports	Investment	Broad money
	(In billions of U.S. dollars)			*(In percent)*			
India	1.38	7.09	8.47	1.6	14.2	7.9	3.2
Neighbors							
Bangladesh	0.54	0.32	0.86	0.2	1.6	1.2	0.4
Pakistan	0.72	...	0.72	0.7	5.2	3.7	1.7
Sri Lanka	0.32	...	0.32	1.5	5.4	5.6	4.7
Other Asia							
China	35.11	6.68	41.79	4.9	20.7	11.2	4.2
Indonesia	4.10	...	4.10	1.4	5.3	4.0	2.9
Korea	−0.91	17.72	16.81	2.4	9.8	6.6	5.6
Philippines	2.71	2.76	5.47	2.5	11.3	10.0	7.5
Thailand	2.22	4.94	7.16	2.7	9.0	7.0	3.3
Latin America							
Argentina	8.57	21.30	29.87	5.6	107.3	28.9	32.3
Brazil	0.30	91.44	91.14	7.9	114.6	39.6	17.4
Mexico	10.48	17.73	28.20	3.9	38.0	16.9	6.9
Europe							
Hungary	3.88	...	3.88	5.3	20.9	26.3	9.8
Turkey	1.22	4.92	6.14	2.8	19.0	2.9	7.8

Source: International Monetary Fund, World Economic Outlook database.

against different sorts of risks. All of these trends served to promote the diversification of international portfolios. On the internal side, foreign investment was attracted to developing countries that have combined dynamic growth performance and prospects with an "investor friendly" environment. Capital inflows were also encouraged by high domestic interest rates relative to international levels. As far as India is concerned the following factors are noteworthy:

- The basic characteristics of the economy were favorable: the existence of well-known corporate names with established track records of performance; reasonably developed stock markets; familiar accounting and legal systems; and the potential for growth implied by a large market, cheap labor, and extensive natural resources.[7]
- The structural reforms launched in 1991 enhanced the growth prospects of the Indian corporate sector. Particularly relevant were the elimination of industrial licensing restrictions, liberalization of the trade regime, and the opening up to the private sector of a number of activities previously reserved for the public sector.

- Liberalization of restrictions on foreign portfolio investment set in motion a process of portfolio adjustment. Foreign investors were aware that the Indian stock exchanges represented about 6 percent of emerging equity market capitalization and 0.7 percent of global equity market capitalization (International Finance Corporation (1994a)).[8] Similarly, reduced restrictions on foreign ownership allowed a number of companies to raise their stakes in joint ventures.
- Domestic firms were encouraged to approach external markets by the low cost of foreign financing relative to domestic financing. This situation reflected (1) the combination of a relatively tight monetary policy with a less restrictive fiscal stance and a heavy overhang of public sector debt that kept domestic borrowing costs high and the external value of the rupee stable, and (2) institutional factors—such as

---

[7]Other South Asian countries may have attracted far less portfolio investment than India because of their generally less well-established corporate sectors and stock markets.

[8]Indian stock markets historically have had relatively low degrees of covariances of returns with other markets, given that the Indian economy is large and relatively closed. The correlation between the Bombay Stock Exchange Sensex index and the S&P 500 in the five years ended March 1994 was 28 percent, lower than most other major emerging markets (International Finance Corporation (1994b)). This low correlation means that Indian stocks can be particularly attractive for risk diversification purposes.

Table 6.7. Sectoral Distribution of Foreign Investment, 1991–94
(In millions of U.S. dollars)

	Net Purchases by FIIs[1]	GDRs[2]		Eurobonds[2]		Foreign Direct Investment[3]	
		Amount	Number	Amount	Number	Amount	Number
Manufacturing	1,447	2,465	35	790	9	3,930	1,569
Basic	528	787	11	655	7	1,611	305
Electricity	126	200	2	—	—	711	7
Mining	57	—	—	—	—	—	—
Capital	164	135	2	100	1	288	468
Consumer	672	1,018	14	—	—	1,199	723
Intermediate	82	45	1	—	—	831	73
Diversified	...	480	7	35	1	...	...
Services	598	140	2	400	3	896	275
Of which:							
Financial	308	—	—	400	3	296	45
Health care	109	—	—	—	—	6	14
Hotels	42	40	1	—	—	232	41
Shipping	47	100	1	—	—	31	18
Telecommunications	92	—	—	—	—	60	27
Diversified[4]	351	519	3	140	1	151	274
Total	2,396	3,124	40	1,330	13	4,977	2,118

Sources: Ministry of Industry; and press reports.
[1]In local exchanges. Through July 27, 1994.
[2]Through October 31, 1994.
[3]Based on approvals data only. Through June 30, 1994.
[4]Figures for net purchase by FIIs and direct foreign investment include investment in the diversified manufacturing company.

minimum bank lending rates, high intermediation costs, and legal requirements for domestic capital issues—that have added to the cost of domestic financing.

Impact on the Economy

Impact on Firms

The recent surge of foreign investment substantially increased the availability of funding to the Indian private sector. Total foreign investment amounted to $5 billion in 1993/94, compared with domestic capital market issues by nongovernment public limited companies of $6.2 billion and disbursements by financial institutions of $8.4 billion (Table 6.7).[9] To a degree, this increased funding was

focused on the leading blue-chip companies: about half of GDR and FCCB issues to date have come from firms in the top 20 (ranked by sales), in industries such as automobiles, chemicals and fertilizers, metallurgical industries, power, and textiles (see Table 6.3).[10] But smaller, fast-growing companies in high-technology areas such as pharmaceuticals have also successfully issued GDRs. FII and foreign direct investment inflows have gone to a much more diverse set of companies across a range of sectors, including the services sector as well as manufacturing (Table 6.8).[11] FII money has been invested in over 500 different companies. While initially interest was mainly in the larger, more liquid stocks, over time attention has shifted to smaller but fast-growing

[9]Secondary market purchases by FIIs ($0.7 billion) are included as foreign investment in this comparison even though the receipts accrue in the first instance to domestic investors rather than to the companies concerned. The inflow from the FIIs created conditions conducive to domestic equity issues, and thus contributed to increasing the availability of funding to Indian companies.

[10]Data for foreign direct investment in Table 6.7 are based on approvals and needs to be treated with caution. For example, actual foreign direct investment flows into the power and telecommunications sectors to date have been very limited.

[11]Note, however, that foreign investment may be geographically quite concentrated. About 75 percent of foreign direct investment approved in 1993/94 was directed at only five states (Maharashtra, Delhi, Orissa, Tamil Nadu, and Madhya Pradesh). These are states that have established a reputation for a business-friendly environment.

Table 6.8. Domestic and External Financing

	1991/92	1992/93	1993/94	1991/92	1992/93	1993/94
	(In millions of U.S. dollars)			*(In percent of GDP)*		
Domestic financing						
Term loans from Indian						
financial institutions[1]	6,466	8,681	8,380	2.6	3.2	3.2
New capital market issues[2]	2,347	7,507	6,217	0.9	2.8	2.4
Equity and preference shares	706	3,779	3,234	0.3	1.4	1.3
Debenture issues	1,641	3,727	2,983	0.7	1.4	1.2
Equity related external financing	148	585	5,104	0.1	0.2	2.0
Foreign direct investment	148	344	620	0.1	0.1	0.2
Foreign portfolio investment	—	242	4,484	—	0.1	1.7
FII inflows	—	1	1,700	—	—	0.7
GDR issues	—	241	1,460	—	0.1	0.6
FCCB issues	—	—	994	—	—	0.4
Other	—	—	330	—	—	0.1
Memorandum item:						
Private investment	35,152	39,005	36,154	14.0	14.6	1.40

Sources: Reserve Bank of India; and IMF staff estimates.

[1]Such as the Industrial Development Bank of India and the Industrial Credit and Investment Corporation of India.

[2]Issues by nongovernment public limited companies.

companies. About 70 percent of the total amount has been invested in the "cash" segment of the Bombay Stock Exchange, which comprises smaller, less liquid stocks.

A key question is to what extent increased access to foreign funds has been used to finance new investments. In principle, GDR issues are related to new investment projects.[12] However, data collected by the Ministry of Finance indicate that through the end of September 1994 only 28 percent of funds raised by companies prior to the imposition of end-use guidelines was used for capital equipment. About 17 percent of the funds had been directed at balance sheet restructuring, in particular, reducing high-cost external and domestic borrowings. The remainder was mainly placed in liquid investments, including unit trusts (which are similar to mutual funds) and government paper. The slow initial response of investment may be attributable to a variety of factors:

First, the timing of fund-raising need not coincide with the timing of use of funds. Firms will tend to raise resources when market conditions are judged to be favorable even if the financing is not required

for some time. Moreover, investment spending will be distributed over time as a project proceeds while fund-raising will be concentrated to minimize transactions costs.

Second, with high domestic interest rates, firms have a legitimate desire to reduce high-cost domestic funding from commercial banks and term lending institutions. Strengthening of the balance sheet is typically a precursor to embarking on major capital investments.

Third, since money is fungible and the inflow of foreign resources is only a fraction of a company's cash flow, end-use restrictions on the deployment of foreign investment may not be very effective. Firms may not have too much difficulty in assigning new foreign investments to capital projects that would be undertaken even in the absence of foreign funding.

There is increasing evidence from production and import data that capital spending grew quite strongly in 1994/95. This would be consistent with strong investment growth stimulated by increased access to foreign financing (and the economic reforms more generally), as capital investment projects move into the implementation phase and as companies complete their balance sheet restructuring.

Macroeconomic Impact

Against the background of a deteriorating fiscal position and slow initial investment response, the im-

---

[12]Euroissue prospectuses describe the intended use for the resources. In almost all cases, this has involved new investment projects. GDR issues approved under the new Finance Ministry guidelines are also required to be used predominantly for capital investment.

Table 6.9. Liquidity Impact of Capital Inflows

	1991/92	1992/93	1993/94	1994/95
	(In millions of U.S. dollars)			
Change in net international reserves	−220	2,582	8,234	4,895
Direct and portfolio investment	148	585	5,104	4,799
	(In billions of rupees)			
Change in reserve money	117.3	112.7	278.4	304.0
Change in net foreign assets	108.6	38.1	287.7	233.0
	(In percent)			
Reserve money growth[1]	13.4	11.3	25.1	21.9
Contribution of net foreign assets[2]	12.4	3.8	26.0	16.8
Memorandum item:				
Broad money growth	19.3	15.7	18.2	21.4

Source: Reserve Bank of India.
[1]Annual rate.
[2]Change in net foreign assets as percent of beginning-period reserve money; annual rate.

mediate impact of the surge in foreign inflows was to generate a rapid increase in domestic liquidity. The counterpart was an accumulation of international reserves as the Reserve Bank intervened to avoid an exchange rate appreciation. To a degree, the increase in liquidity may have made it easier for companies that did not have direct access to international markets to fund their own investment projects through banks or the capital markets. However, the easing of credit conditions is also likely to have contributed to higher consumption (for example, as firms' resistance to wage pressures was relaxed), rising inflation, and an appreciation of the real exchange rate.

The scale of the initial impact on liquidity can be seen from the fact that the $8.2 billion increase in net foreign assets of the Reserve Bank in 1993/94 corresponded to 26 percent of reserve money at the start of the year (Table 6.9). Although not the only factor, foreign investment flows accounted for a substantial part of this increase. Open market operations totaling $2.9 billion mitigated the effects of the large fiscal deficit, but were insufficient to contain the monetary impact of the rapid accumulation of foreign assets. Reserve money increased by 25 percent, inflation rose from 7 percent in March 1993 to about 12 percent in March 1994, and the real effective exchange rate appreciated by about 4 percent.

In 1994/95, with efforts to correct the fiscal slippage and with a growing recovery of investment, capital inflows were absorbed more easily. The moderation in the rate of inflows, together with a widening in the trade deficit as the economic recovery gathered momentum, contributed to a slowing in the rate of growth of net foreign assets. Steps to tighten monetary policy—including a hike in cash reserve requirements—and the limited expansion of net Reserve Bank credit to the government as the fiscal position improved also helped to dampen money growth. Inflation remained in double digits for most of 1994/95 but came down toward the end of the year as the monetary tightening took effect. The real effective exchange rate also depreciated, as the U.S. dollar weakened against third countries.

Interestingly, so far the capital inflows have not had a marked impact on the current account of the balance of payments. The current account deficit in fact contracted from 2 percent of GDP in 1992/93 to virtual balance in 1993/94. A small deficit (about $1/2$ of 1 percent of GDP) was recorded in 1994/95. To a degree, this moderate response may be attributable to the still relatively closed nature of the Indian economy, particularly the heavily protected consumer goods sector; stronger domestic demand did not immediately lead to higher imports. However, the current account deficit is likely to widen as imports pick up and exports are diverted to the domestic market.

Impact on Financial Markets

To date, the impact of foreign capital flows on Indian financial markets has been more qualitative than quantitative. Total FII investment on Indian stock exchanges is considerably less than 5 percent of market capitalization, and FII transactions have not exceeded 10 percent of market turnover in any single month. The introduction of foreign investment in Indian equity has not added significantly to market liquidity or to the volatility of stock prices.[13] Nevertheless, the presence of FIIs in Indian markets has probably contributed to a process that was already under way—the growing role of the wholesale capital market and the evolution of the institutions and financial structures to support it.

Historically, the Indian capital market has been essentially retail based. There are a large number of stocks (over 3,000 companies are listed on the Bombay Stock Exchange), a large number of investors (by one estimate, there are 30 million shareholders), small lot sizes, and a multitude of small intermediaries other than the major publicly owned financial institutions such as the Unit Trust of India. The development of secondary markets has been hampered by limited liquidity and cumbersome transfer and settlement procedures. Elements of a modern financial system have begun to emerge recently, including the growing importance of investment banking activities and the emergence of private mutual funds. The FIIs have added another group of institutional investors with sophisticated needs and concerns. This has given additional momentum to efforts to improve market efficiency and transparency, including to overhaul settlement and transfer systems, introduce screen-based trading, tighten regulatory safeguards, and introduce new financial instruments such as derivatives for better risk management.

A particular question is whether the emergence of an offshore market in Indian equity—the GDR market—has had a significant impact on domestic markets in the underlying shares, as has occurred elsewhere. For example, following the launching of a $3 billion GDR program, shares in the Mexican telephone company—Telmex—are mainly traded on the New York Stock Exchange, and prices on the Mexican Bolsa de Valores follow in step. However, to date links between the offshore market for Indian GDRs and local markets have been limited. Substantial discounts or premiums of GDR prices relative to local prices have tended to persist over time, particularly for the smaller companies (Chart 6.3). Moreover, GDR prices of Indian companies have tended to be more volatile than the prices of those companies on the Bombay Stock Exchange (Chart 6.4). As

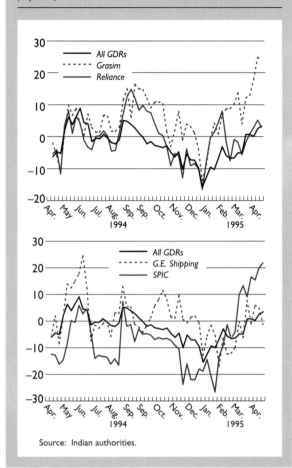

Chart 6.3. Discounts or Premiums of GDR Prices Relative to Prices on the Bombay Stock Exchange
(In percent)

Source: Indian authorities.

shown in Chart 6.5, an upward movement of prices on the Bombay Stock Exchange has tended to be associated with an increase in the GDR price relative to the Bombay Stock Exchange price, and vice versa.

The principal reason why arbitrage does not lead to price convergence relates to the high transactions costs involved in moving between the markets: liquidity in both markets is low; there are considerable settlement risks in buying or selling shares on local markets; registration of shares can take three months or more; and the process of converting a GDR into its underlying shares is cumbersome. Arbitrage is further limited by the fact that the investor base for the two markets is segmented. Only approved FIIs are players in both markets, and their willingness to arbitrage is affected by tax laws that favor holding periods of greater than one year.

---

[13]In a cross-country study of emerging markets, Aziz (1995) reports that Indian stock price volatility has increased since FIIs have been permitted to participate. However, this conclusion is based on a very broad time comparison: the period 1976–May 1992 compared with the period June 1992–February 1994. If one looks at a shorter time span, the opposite seems to be the case: price volatility has declined since mid-1992 compared with the previous two and a half years (see Chart 6.1). A number of factors, however, may account for this decline other than the opening of the market. Thus, firm conclusions should not be drawn from this observation.

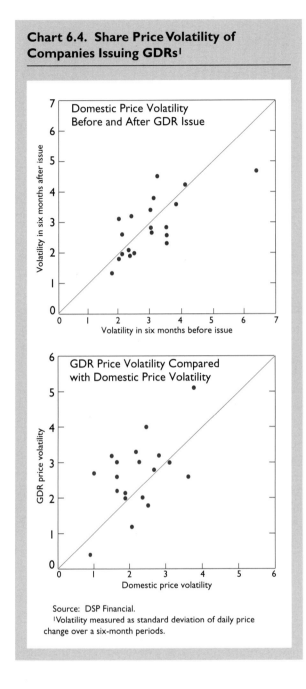

Chart 6.4. Share Price Volatility of Companies Issuing GDRs[1]

Domestic Price Volatility Before and After GDR Issue

Volatility in six months after issue

Volatility in six months before issue

GDR Price Volatility Compared with Domestic Price Volatility

GDR price volatility

Domestic price volatility

Source: DSP Financial.
[1]Volatility measured as standard deviation of daily price change over a six-month periods.

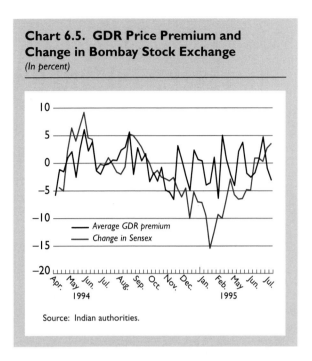

Chart 6.5. GDR Price Premium and Change in Bombay Stock Exchange
(In percent)

Average GDR premium
Change in Sensex

Apr. May Jun. Jul. Aug. Sep. Oct. Nov. Dec. Jan. Feb. May Jun. Jul.
1994   1995

Source: Indian authorities.

Sustainability of Capital Flows

It seems unlikely that equity portfolio flows will soon return to the rates experienced in late 1993/94 to early 1994/95 as institutional investors reappraise the risks of investing in emerging markets. Nevertheless, the prospects are still favorable that, with sensible macroeconomic and reform policies that foster strong growth and capital market development, India will continue to attract substantial, even rising, levels of private capital inflows.

The desire to diversify portfolios will continue to encourage foreign portfolio investment into India, both through direct purchases on local exchanges and through GDR issues. Market reforms to improve transparency and efficiency of trading—including the spread of screen-based trading and the setup of a centralized depository system—would also help to sustain these flows by making the Indian market more attractive.

Direct foreign investment will become increasingly important. The rate of such inflows has increased markedly in 1995. Such investment should rise dramatically with increased private involvement in infrastructure projects in the telecommunications and power sectors, once appropriate frameworks have been established in these sectors (see Section VII). External commercial borrowing will also continue, particularly in financing infrastructure projects.

VII Structural Reforms and the Implications for Investment and Growth

Ajai Chopra, Woosik Chu, and Oliver Fratzscher

Since 1991, India has introduced major reforms to improve the efficiency of resource allocation and expand the productive capacity of the economy. These reforms have focused on liberalizing product markets, particularly by removing impediments to private investment (both domestic and foreign), and liberalizing the trade and external payments regimes. The liberalization of factor markets has so far centered on financial markets, with emphasis on increasing the role of market mechanisms in the allocation of credit.

Although the reforms are by no means complete, much has been accomplished and the private sector's response has been positive. However, obstacles to a stronger and broader investment response remain. Despite efforts to attract private investment, inadequate infrastructure is still a major constraint, preventing industry from committing itself to large-scale investments. Moreover, in other areas—such as public enterprises, labor market and exit policies, and the agricultural sector—little has been done as yet to address serious distortions.

This section focuses on four areas of reform: (1) the external trade regime;[1] (2) the investment regime; (3) public enterprises; and (4) the financial sector. The issue of labor markets and exit policies is discussed in the context of both industrial policy and public enterprises. The progress in reducing distortions and changing incentives is discussed, and the initial outcome of the reforms is assessed. The major remaining structural impediments and the unfinished agenda for reforms are highlighted.

Trade Reform

For most of the postindependence period, India's trade policy was largely geared toward self-reliance through import-substitution policies. Quantitative restrictions were pervasive, and import tariffs were extremely high. There were also numerous other restrictions on trade as outlined in Table 7.1. Direct restrictions on exports, a protected domestic market with a high cost structure, and restricted access to inputs for export production resulted in a strong antiexport bias. Heavy protection, together with restrictions on foreign investment that limited opportunities for adopting new technology and learning by doing, also fostered low productivity and inefficient domestic industries.

The trade reforms undertaken since 1991 have reduced substantially the antiexport bias of Indian industry. The level and dispersion of tariffs have been cut sharply and quantitative restrictions have been eased. These reforms were preceded by a substantial devaluation of the rupee, which led to a 15 percent depreciation of the real effective exchange rate between 1991 and 1992. The real effective exchange rate has remained essentially unchanged since then. These policies, together with industrial delicensing and a more liberal foreign investment regime, contributed to strong export growth in 1993/94 and 1994/95. Nevertheless, India's trade regime remains one of the most protected in Asia and progress in trade liberalization lags behind most other developing economies.

Progress in Reducing Distortions

The maximum tariff was lowered from 400 percent in 1990/91 to 110 percent in 1992/93, and most recently to 50 percent in 1995/96. Average (import-weighted) tariffs have been reduced from 87 percent in 1990/91 to 27 percent in 1994/95 (Table 7.2). Both the nominal and effective rates of protection have come down sharply, with capital goods facing the lowest effective rate (39 percent in 1994/95) and consumer goods the highest (81 percent).[2] With efforts to achieve a more uniform tariff structure, tariff dispersion—as measured by standard deviations—has fallen from 41 percent in 1990/91 to 21 percent in 1995/96. In addition, the gradual elimination of tariff exemptions has narrowed the gap between the average tariff and the collection rate: a gap of some

---

[1]Tariff reductions have been closely connected with tax reforms, which were discussed in Section V.

[2]Estimates of effective protection are from the World Bank (1994).

Table 7.1. Trade Policy Reform: Progress to Date and Future Reform Areas

Status Before July 1991	Status in Mid-1995	Areas of Future Reform
Import restrictions Quantitative restrictions on 91 percent of value added of all tradables (90 percent of value added of manufacturing); import licensing based on 26 separate lists.	Most quantitative restrictions on import of capital and intermediate goods eliminated and a single negative list established. Quantitative restrictions on 75 percent of value added of all tradables still maintained, but reduced to 51 percent of value added of manufactured goods. Limited import of consumer goods possible through open general license scheme, special import license scheme, and consumer goods imported as baggage.	Phase out remaining quantitative restrictions on imports, replacing these with appropriate tariffs. Liberalize consumer goods imports.
Import of 55 goods "canalized" (i.e., restricted to import by state agencies).	Most items unrestricted.	Free remaining items, including petroleum and agricultural products, together with rationalization of pricing, distribution, and subsidization of the respective industries.
Other nontariff barriers: Actual user policy, phased manufacturing program, and government purchase preferences.	Abolished.	
Tariffs Maximum rate: 400 percent Average (import-weighted): 87 percent Dispersion (standard deviation): 41 percent Rate of effective protection: 164 percent (manufacturing).	Maximum rate: 50 percent Average (import-weighted): 27 percent Dispersion (standard deviation): 21 percent Rate of effective protection: 72 percent (manufacturing).	Further cuts in tariffs and reduction in dispersion.
Export controls 439 items of various product categories subject to controls.	Export controls partially lifted. Items subject to controls were reduced to 210 (1993/94), the remaining items are mostly agricultural products and minerals.	Decontrol remaining items including agricultural products and minerals.
Export taxes Export taxes levied on some mineral and agricultural items.	Abolished.	
Export subsidies Direct subsidies targeting specific sectors.	Export subsidies streamlined. Direct subsidies are being gradually eliminated and sector-specific subsidies are replaced by more general schemes such as not taxing export profits and duty drawback schemes.	Phase out as import tariffs are reduced and local costs are lowered.

45 percentage points in 1990/91 was reduced to 19 percentage points by 1993/94.

With the elimination of import licensing requirements for intermediate and capital goods, the share of value added subject to quantitative restrictions in the manufacturing sector decreased from about 90 percent in the pre-reform period to 51 percent in 1994/95 (Table 7.2). The inclusion of more consumer goods in the open general license list starting in 1995/96 is expected to lower this figure further.

Nevertheless, imports of consumer goods remain severely restricted. Quantitative restrictions on agricultural imports are also still pervasive, covering over 90 percent of value added as of 1994/95.

Restrictions on exports have been relaxed, with the number of restricted items falling from 439 in March 1990 to 210 in March 1994. The remaining restrictions are mostly in the agricultural and mining sectors. Along with the elimination of export restrictions, various export incentive schemes have been

Table 7.2. Effects of the Reform on Trade Regime
(End of period; in percent, unless otherwise indicated)

	1990/91	1992/93	1993/94	Est. 1994/95	Proj. 1995/96
Tariffs					
Maximum tariffs	400	110	85	65	50
Average tariffs (unweighted)	128	94	71	55	42
Average tariffs (import weighted)	87	64	47	33	27
Dispersion (standard deviation)	41	34	30	25	21
Collection rate	42	32	28	...	...
Rate of protection (value-added weighted)					
Effective rate of protection					
Intermediate goods	148	114	90	71	...
Capital goods	87	70	46	39	...
Consumer goods	192	125	97	81	...
Total manufacturing	164	114	88	72	...
Nominal rate of protection					
Intermediate goods	125	100	77	55	...
Capital goods	106	82	57	43	...
Consumer goods	137	99	75	59	...
Total manufacturing	129	97	73	55	...
Quantitative restriction					
Items subject to import licensing (share of value added)					
Agriculture	93	...	...	93	...
Mining	100	...	...	45	...
Manufacturing	90	...	...	51	...
All tradables	91	...	...	75	...
Number of items subject to export restrictions	439	...	210	...	...

Sources: Data provided by the Indian authorities; and the World Bank.

revamped to streamline procedures and reduce distortions, while sector-specific direct export subsidies have essentially been eliminated.

The Impact on the Economy

The economy has reacted positively to the reduction in trade distortions and change in relative prices. The country is now more open, with the ratio of total trade to GDP rising from an average of 12.7 percent in the 1980s to nearly 19 percent in 1994/95 (Table 7.3).[3] Furthermore, the premium on smuggled goods has been reduced sharply.

Export volumes increased by an average of nearly 19 percent a year in 1993/94 and 1994/95, after a weak performance in the previous two years (Table 7.4). This strong performance was spurred by the depreciation of the real exchange rate and a reduction in the antiexport bias of the trade system. The export surge has affected a broad range of products, both manufactured and agricultural. Thus, a major shift in the composition of exports is not yet evident.[4]

Imports contracted sharply in 1991/92 owing to the imposition of administrative controls, but rebounded strongly in 1992/93. With the increasing momentum of economic activity, imports rose markedly in 1994/95, with non-oil imports growing by over 30 percent. Imports of capital and export-related items still account for a large proportion of imports, with imports of consumer goods still quite limited.

Future Priorities

Notwithstanding the progress in reforming the trade regime, tariffs and the rate of protection in India are much higher than those of East Asian economies, and indeed of many developing coun-

---

[3]These changes cannot be attributed to trade reform and exchange rate policy alone. Cyclical and exogenous events have also likely played a role.

[4]For example, ready-made garments and handicrafts still accounted for about 16 percent of total exports in the first half of 1994/95, essentially unchanged from the late 1980s.

Table 7.3. Exports and Imports Relative to GDP
(In percent)

	Average 1981/92– 1990/91	1990/91	1991/92	1992/93	1993/94	Est. 1994/95
Exports/GDP	5.0	6.0	7.1	7.6	8.9	9.1
Imports/GDP	7.7	8.1	7.8	9.0	9.3	9.8
Total trade/GDP	12.7	14.1	14.9	16.7	18.2	18.8

Source: Ministry of Finance, *Economic Survey*, various issues.

tries (Table 7.5). To a degree, concerns about the loss of revenue have affected the pace of tariff reductions. There have also been concerns about the ability of certain industries to adjust to increased competition, which has led to higher tariffs for some sectors and effective rates of protection may even have risen in some instances.[5]

The main tasks remaining are the elimination of quantitative restrictions and a further reduction of tariff levels. As long as imports of consumer goods remain heavily constrained, the danger of misallocation of investment and lack of competition will be serious and India's performance in what could be a dynamic sector will remain subdued.[6] Replacing the ban on the import of these goods with appropriate tariffs would also raise revenue, which would strengthen the fiscal situation. Restrictions on trade in agricultural goods also need to be lifted to allow this sector greater opportunity to compete in world markets.[7] Along with the reduction of tariff levels, variations depending on the types of goods, sectors, and end uses should be reduced so as to make the tariff structure more uniform.

The Investment Regime

Prior to the middle of 1991, private investment was not permitted in many key sectors of the econ-

omy. In areas where such investment was allowed, a complex web of regulations and licensing requirements inhibited productivity and growth. Over the past four years, major steps have been taken to liberalize India's investment regime and dismantle the system of controls. This section reviews progress of reforms in five key areas (see also Table 7.6): (1) deregulation of the industrial sector; (2) upgrading of infrastructure; (3) reforms of exit policies to reduce labor and property market rigidities; (4) liberalization of the foreign investment regime; and (5) agricultural reform.

Deregulation of the Industrial Sector

The deregulation of the industrial sector has been an important element of the reforms initiated in the middle of 1991. Until then, India was one of the most heavily regulated economies in the world. Domestic competition was hindered by licensing, which limited entry, changes in product mix, and the expansion of successful firms. In addition to licensing requirements, the Monopolies and Restrictive Trade Practices Act placed further barriers to expansion for large firms. Industrial efficiency was also undermined by preferences granted to public enterprises, policies that encouraged excessive capital intensity, administered prices, and a regional price equalization scheme that discouraged geographic specialization.

These policies led to a number of highly protected manufacturing industries with low efficiency. During the 1980s, protected industries (such as petroleum, coal, chemicals, steel, and fertilizers) accounted for over half of fixed capital formation in manufacturing, but contributed only about two fifths of the sector's value added. Moreover, these industries were three times as capital intensive and twice as power intensive as those industries with low protection.

---

[5]For example, tariffs were typically reduced faster on capital goods than on the ferrous metals used to manufacture these products.

[6]As noted earlier, there has not yet been much diversification in the structure of exports. In contrast to a number of successful Asian economies, India has not significantly expanded exports of light consumer goods such as toys, watches, electronics, and computers.

[7]For example, quantitative restrictions were imposed in 1994 on coffee exports to protect the domestic market at a time of a sharp rise in global prices.

Table 7.4. Effects of the Reform on Trade

	1990/91	1991/92	1992/93	1993/94	Est. 1994/95
	(In billions of U.S. dollars; balance of payments)				
Trade volume					
Exports, f.o.b.	18.5	18.3	18.9	22.7	26.8
Imports, c.i.f.	27.9	21.1	23.2	24.0	30.3
Total trade	46.4	39.3	42.1	46.7	57.1
	(Percent change)				
Exports, f.o.b.	9.0	−1.1	3.3	20.3	17.4
Imports, c.i.f.	14.3	−24.5	10.3	3.2	23.1
Total trade	12.2	−15.2	7.1	10.9	20.4
	(In percent of exports and imports; customs)				
Trade structure					
Principal commodities					
Exports					
Primary products	23.8	23.1	20.9	22.0	...
Manufactured goods	71.6	73.6	75.7	74.9	...
Textile fabrics and manufactures	20.8	22.4	23.2	21.3	...
Handicrafts	18.9	19.0	20.4	21.5	...
Minerals and lubricants	2.9	2.3	2.6	1.8	...
Others	1.7	1.0	0.8	1.3	...
Imports					
Bulk imports	45.6	44.8	44.9	39.2	...
Nonbulk imports	54.4	55.2	55.1	60.8	...
Capital goods	24.2	21.8	20.7	26.0	...
Mainly export-related items	15.3	18.4	19.0	19.0	...
Others	14.9	15.0	15.4	15.7	...
Direction of trade					
Exports					
OECD	53.5	57.9	60.5	56.9	58.8
OPEC	5.6	8.7	9.6	10.7	9.2
Eastern Europe	17.9	10.9	4.4	3.8	3.6
Asia	14.3	14.8	17.4	20.7	20.0
Others	8.7	7.7	8.1	7.9	8.4
Imports					
OECD	54.0	54.2	56.1	56.2	51.1
OPEC	16.3	19.9	21.6	22.4	21.4
Eastern Europe	7.8	5.1	2.5	1.8	2.4
Asia	14.0	11.2	10.5	12.1	14.1
Others	7.9	9.6	9.3	8.0	11.0
Memorandum items:					
Current account					
(In billions of U.S. dollars)	−10.1	−1.6	−3.9	−0.6	−1.4
(In percent of GDP)	−3.4	−0.7	−1.6	−0.3	0.5
Real effective exchange rate					
(change in percent; end of period)	−8.7	−24.2	−3.2	3.8	−5.1

Sources: Data provided by the Indian authorities; Ministry of Finance, *Economic Survey*, various issues; Reserve Bank of India, *Annual Report*, various issues; and IMF staff estimates.

Deregulation and decontrol measures have included (1) removing investment licensing requirements in most industrial sectors, leaving only a few areas (for example, petroleum, coal, and agroprocessing) still subject to these requirements; (2) amending antitrust legislation to eliminate the restraints to large firms' expansion, diversification, merger, and acquisition; (3) gradually reducing the areas reserved for the public sector; and (4) eliminating many price controls, for example on steel, aluminum, and cement.

The reforms have energized the Indian private sector. Investment picked up markedly in 1994/95, and output in most sectors is increasing rapidly (see

Table 7.5. International Comparison of Openness
(In percent)

Country	Maximum Tariff[1]	Average Tariff[1,2]	Total Trade/GDP (1994)[3]
Argentina	20	11	13
Brazil	35	15	12
Chile	15	11	43
Egypt	80	42	31
Ghana	25	12	52
India[4]	65	55	19
Indonesia	40	22	46
Korea	30	10	49
Malaysia	40	14	156
Mexico	20	20	27
Morocco	35	23	35
Philippines	50	26	54
Thailand	60	14	68

Sources: Kirmani and others (1994); and IMF staff estimates.

[1]Based on information available in May 1994.

[2]Unweighted average.

[3]Merchandise trade only; hence figures for India differ from Table 5.3, which are for exports and imports of goods and non-factor services.

[4]For comparability, the figures shown for India are those applicable in May 1994. In the 1995/96 budget, the maximum tariff was lowered to 50 percent and the unweighted average tariff is now estimated to be 42 percent.

Section III for details). Investment in such areas as automobiles and consumer electronics has been particularly strong.[8] In other areas, such as telecommunications, power, petrochemicals, and oil exploration, major investments are being planned, although the process is slow (see below on infrastructure policies). However, a number of obstacles remain. First, concerns about the ability of public enterprises to compete have continued to impede private activity in some areas.[9] Second, the process of obtaining all the necessary licenses and permits at the state level is still extremely cumbersome.[10] A third obstacle is the continued policy of reserving production of some 850 items (including most non-durable consumer products) for small-scale enterprises. Small-scale industries also receive purchase and price preferences, subsidized loans, tax exemptions at the state level, and protection through the quantitative restrictions on imports of many consumer goods. Nevertheless, the inability to exploit economies of scale has inhibited investment, innovation, and production efficiency in sectors where India should have considerable export potential.[11]

Infrastructure Policies

The poor quality of India's infrastructure (especially in power, roads, water, and telecommunications) is likely to be a major obstacle to India's economic development in the coming years.[12] Most existing infrastructure facilities are state monopolies. Although public investment in infrastructure has been substantial in recent years (an estimated 43 percent of total public investment planned for 1991–96), provision of infrastructure has suffered from poor financial management, operational inefficiency, and inadequate maintenance.

The authorities have recognized the advantages of private sector investment in these sectors, to provide both financing and technical expertise. In principle, all these sectors have been opened to private participation. However, notwithstanding considerable private sector interest, actual progress has been slow so far for a number of institutional and financial reasons. First, attracting infrastructure investment requires an appropriate licensing and regulatory framework. The process of establishing these frameworks has been slow and key regulatory and administrative arrangements are still in the process of being established. For example, the deadline for bids to provide both basic and cellular telephone services had to be extended while the government replied to numerous queries from potential bidders on issues such as interconnectivity of public and private networks, the intended regulatory regime, and revenue sharing.[13] Second, a viable commercial framework must be established. Investment in the power sector has been limited by concerns about the solvency of the main purchasers, the state electricity

---

[8]Software has been a special success story as Indian firms have taken advantage of low-cost, highly skilled workers and technological advances that have allowed programming activity to be decentralized from its point of use.

[9]For example, in civil aviation, the expansion of private activity has been slowed by regulatory constraints apparently because of concerns for the implications for publicly owned carriers as well as strains on infrastructural capacity.

[10]See Confederation of Indian Industry (1994) for a compendium of various clearances (for example, for land acquisition, electricity and water connections, and sales tax registration) that must be obtained from state governments to set up an industry.

[11]Some progress has been made in relaxing reservation policies where an export commitment is made. For example, in the garments industry investment up to Rs 30 million is allowed if a company exports 50 percent of its output. The reservation policy has also been relaxed on a case-by-case basis if an export commitment of 75 percent of output is provided.

[12]See World Bank (1995) for a thorough survey of issues in this area.

[13]The results of a first round of auctions for licenses for cellular services had to be quashed because of legal challenges to the system for allocating licenses.

Table 7.6. Industrial Policy Reform: Progress to Date and Medium-Term Objectives

Status in 1991	Progress Through Mid-1995	Areas of Future Reform
Deregulation policies Government licenses required for about 60 percent of new investment.	Licensing abolished for all but 15 sectors.	Further prune the list and eliminate state and local restrictions.
Expansion of larger firms tightly controlled.	Antitrust legislation amended to free decisions relating to expansion and diversification.	
Eighteen major areas reserved exclusively for the public sector.	The list of areas reserved for the public sector has been gradually reduced.	
Reservation policy: protection of small-scale production with list of 850 reserved products.	Some exemptions in export-oriented industries.	Further pruning of reserved products list.
Infrastructure and foreign direct investment policies Infrastructure remains major impediment to growth. Limited scope for foreign direct investment, based on lengthy case-by-case consideration; foreign equity limited to 40 percent.	Policy frameworks established for investment in infrastructure. Automatic approval for up to 51 percent foreign equity holding in 34 selected areas. Other approval procedures simplified. Restriction on use of brand names eliminated.	Establish or clarify regulatory and administrative arrangements for infrastructure investment. Expand coverage of automatic approval of foreign direct investment.
Exit policies Board of Industrial and Financial Restructuring (BIFR) charged with handling exit of private sector firms, but referrals only made when firms are already chronically sick. Slow follow-up.	Limited strengthening of BIFR, including stiffer criteria used to assess viability.	Early referral to BIFR, further strengthening of BIFR procedures for liquidation, and comprehensive legal reforms at center and state levels.
Urban Land Ceiling and Regulation Act (ULCRA) regulates liquidation of land assets.	No change.	Reforming ULCRA by legalizing exemptions and waiving ceilings for restructuring purposes.
Industrial Disputes Act prohibits closure, layoffs, and retrenchment for all plants employing 100 or more workers without government approval.	No change.	Eliminate requirement that government approve labor force reductions and provide greater room for bilateral negotiation between management and workers.

boards.[14] Third, there are issues of financing: a more mature debt market with a longer-term segment needs to be developed, and ways need to be found to tap small savers and appropriate forms of foreign financing.[15]

---

[14]In 1994, the central government identified power projects as a key target for private sector investment and agreed to provide counterguarantees to a limited number of projects to "jump-start" the process. The counterguarantees by the central government would ensure payments by state electricity boards. These boards are to set electricity rates on a cost-plus basis sufficient to yield a guaranteed rate of return on equity of about 16 percent. Some state governments have started to privatize the distribution process, thus increasing the security of returns to investment.

[15]Discussions on alternative financing schemes are under way. One option being considered is some type of postal savings, which has been successfully implemented in Japan, channeling small savers' funds to a variety of infrastructure projects.

Exit Policies

The terms "industrial sickness" and "exit policy" are peculiar to the Indian situation. Industrial sickness refers to public and private enterprises that chronically make losses but continue to operate. Exit policy refers to regulatory policies that block the liquidation of these loss-making enterprises.

The Goswami Committee report (1993) points out several reasons for the phenomenon of industrial sickness:[16] (1) the focus in the financial system (at least until 1991) on maximizing loans for industrial

---

[16]See also Anant and others (1994) for a discussion of the institutional background that gave rise to industrial sickness.

development;[17] (2) weak banking supervision that allowed continued lending to overleveraged and undervalued companies through interest capitalization; (3) substandard management, compounded by inadequate monitoring and supervision by shareholders, who were often dominated by public financial institutions; and (4) legal obstacles to restructuring, with considerable interference by state and local authorities. Thus, although industrial sickness is often associated with surplus labor, other factors have been at least as important constraints to efficiency.

Progress on institutional reforms to provide for restructuring of sick companies has been slow. A quasi-judicial body, the Board of Industrial and Financial Restructuring (BIFR), was created in 1987 as a fast facilitation agency to frame restructuring and bankruptcy packages based on careful consultation among interested parties.[18] The BIFR now deals with both public and private chronically sick enterprises. However, its procedures have proven to be extremely slow moving and have not provided a mechanism for efficient restructuring.[19] Moreover, even after the BIFR has reached a decision, impediments remain. Thus, due to elaborate legal procedures, none of the 150 cases where the BIFR has recommended closure has yet been shut down.

The restructuring of sick companies has also been difficult because of inflexible labor laws (the Industrial Disputes Act), which require firms employing more than 100 workers to obtain prior approval of the state government to retrench labor.[20] Similarly, under existing property laws (the Urban Land Ceiling and Regulation Act), firms are unable to sell urban land and liquidate assets or use the resources for restructuring without state approval. These rigid labor and property laws mean that firms are unable to restructure or close even though they are effectively bankrupt, while also impeding the adjustment

of the economy in response to changing economic conditions.[21] Labor market rigidities also encourage excessive capital intensity in the organized sector.[22] In addition, the combination of rigid property laws and tight rent controls have led to enormous misallocation of land. For example, property values in Bombay are among the highest in the world.

A workable exit policy for unviable units will require an overhaul of labor and land use legislation to ensure flexibility of factor use, as well as major changes in the BIFR mechanism.[23] It will be particularly important to provide greater room for free bilateral negotiation between management and workers, without requiring that the government approve any labor force reduction before it can occur. Such steps would need to be backed up by an adequate social safety net to ameliorate the transitional costs. The National Renewal Fund (established in 1991) already provides resources that can be used for voluntary retirement schemes for public units, but the scope for the fund would need to be broadened for it to become more effective.

Policies on Foreign Direct Investment

The liberalization of the foreign investment regime has been another major advance in India's industrial policy since 1991. Key measures include (1) allowing up to 51 percent foreign participation in 35 high-priority industries on an automatic approval basis, with the possibility of approval up to 100 percent on a case-by-case basis;[24] (2) streamlining government approval procedures with a fast-track mechanism even where the automatic route cannot be used; and (3) preferential tax rates and tax holidays, bilateral investment treaties, and accession to the Multilateral Investment Guarantee Agency.

Between 1991 and March 1995, a cumulative $6 billion of foreign direct investment had been approved. However, just over $2 billion has actually materialized, a large proportion of which consists of increased equity shares in existing joint ventures rather than new projects. This slow response partly indicates the normal lags involved in launching new projects. However, a large number of disincentives

---

[17]Bank credit to sick companies has risen steadily. By 1992, the total had reached Rs 84 billion in over 2,000 large and medium-sized sick private enterprises and Rs 31 billion in over 250,000 small-sized sick private firms. Textile and engineering industries have been two major problem areas. Ahluwalia (1995) reports that the performance of public sector enterprises has been even worse. About 58 chronic loss-making central government enterprises accumulated losses of Rs 99 billion compared with their paid-up capital of Rs 30 billion, while more than 500 chronic loss-making state government enterprises have accumulated losses of Rs 20 billion compared with a paid-up capital of Rs 23 billion.

[18]As discussed below, income recognition norms for banks have also been tightened and banking supervision has been strengthened.

[19]See Anant and others (1994). During the period July 1987 to July 1992, 44 percent of the 1,014 cases referred to the BIFR remained undecided.

[20]As a result, only a tiny fraction (about 3 percent) of India's labor force is employed in the private organized sector. About 7 percent is employed in the public sector.

[21]For example, the transfer of resources from import-competing sectors to the export sector in response to trade reform would be impeded by present labor laws.

[22]Despite rapid growth in output in the private organized sector in the 1980s, there was virtually no increase in employment over this period. See International Labor Organization (1993).

[23]The Goswami Committee report on industrial sickness made a number of relevant recommendations that have not yet been acted upon (Goswami and others (1993)).

[24]The limit is 40 percent in all other industries (except 24 percent in small-scale sectors); in these cases as well, up to 100 percent foreign equity is permitted on a case-by-case basis.

remain. Apart from the constraints noted earlier, foreign investors are particularly concerned by perceived political interference in screening proposed investments and a slow-moving legal system. Also, unlike some other countries, privatization has progressed slowly and has not involved substantial foreign participation.

Agricultural Reform

India has devoted considerable resources to agricultural and rural development over the past three decades. The spread of irrigation, fertilizers, and high-yielding seed varieties has led to a "green revolution" in parts of the country and has alleviated food shortages. Despite these successes, important restrictions on agricultural activity inhibit the development of this key sector of the economy. These restrictions include licensing requirements in agroprocessing industries; restrictions on agricultural exports; and barriers to internal trade and storage. Extensive controls on commerce in agricultural products, together with input price distortions, have reduced incentives for producers and inhibited productivity growth.[25] As a result, labor productivity in India's farm sector has grown by an average of $1/2$ of 1 percent a year over the past two decades, compared with productivity growth in East Asian farming of over 2 percent a year. Much of the increase in food production has been due to an extension of cropped areas, supported by costly subsidies that are no longer sustainable. Low productivity has contributed to slow growth of farm wages and persistent poverty in rural areas.

Liberalization of agricultural policies has the potential for dynamic, labor-intensive growth that would be conducive to a more rapid spread of the benefits of reform.[26] The first priority should be to dismantle the pervasive controls on agricultural commerce, in the way the industrial sector was deregulated in 1991. This would involve eliminating licensing requirements for wholesale trade and storage, phasing out public sector procurement, abolishing the remaining controls on imports and exports of many agricultural items, and ending the licensing of agroprocessing industries. Second, the system of price incentives should mirror market conditions. The resources presently devoted to farm subsidies could be better spent on rural infrastructure development, particularly transport, storage, and rural credit systems.

Public Enterprise Reform

Although the private sector has been invigorated by the reform process, the large public enterprise sector remains a drag on the economy.[27] There has been some success in lowering the budgetary cost of this sector, but public enterprises continue to suffer from low profitability and limited managerial autonomy. Public enterprises have often not been in a position to respond forcefully to increasing competition from the private sector in many areas, resulting in continued inefficient use of a large part of India's capital and labor force.

Public Sector Performance

The public sector's share in GDP increased from about 8 percent in 1960 to over 25 percent in 1993/94. In 1994, India had more than 1,000 public enterprises, about 800 of which were owned by the states.[28] About 240 nonfinancial central government enterprises employ about 2.2 million people and account for about 13 percent of GDP. Public enterprises continue to dominate industries such as coal mining and energy (close to 100 percent share), nonferrous metals (over 80 percent), steel (over 60 percent), and fertilizers (about 40 percent).[29] The public sector's share of output in basic metals and machinery sectors remained above 25 percent in 1994, whereas it was about 15 percent in manufacturing.[30] Public enterprises are generally highly capital intensive: in the manufacturing sector, at the end of the 1980s the public sector accounted for 55 percent of total investment but only 15 percent of total output.[31]

The financial performance of public enterprises is poor and has not improved much in recent years. Gross profit over capital employed was about 11 percent in central public enterprises in 1993/94, compared with nearly 20 percent in the private sector.[32] After taxes, net profits of public enterprises amounted to less than 3 percent of employed capital, which in most cases was insufficient to cover depreciation (Table 7.7). Although the petroleum sector remains profitable, public enterprises show negative profit margins in many sectors (for example, tex-

---

[25]Heavily subsidized fertilizers and electricity on the one hand, and implicit taxation through trade restrictions and domestic price intervention on the other, have created a complex web of distortions.

[26]See Pursell and Gulati (1993) for a discussion of the agenda for agricultural reform.

[27]For a more extensive discussion see Mohan (1995).

[28]State electricity boards and state transport boards account for a large share of state public enterprises' assets and production. Other state public enterprises are considerably smaller and of much less economic significance than the central public enterprises.

[29]See Ministry of Industry (1995).

[30]The share in manufacturing refers to output share of central public enterprises in organized and unorganized manufacturing.

[31]See Ahluwalia (1995). These figures not only indicate capital intensity, but also inefficiency.

[32]See Ahluwalia (1995).

Table 7.7. Profitability of Central Government Public Enterprises
(In billions of rupees, unless otherwise noted)

	1990/91	1991/92	1992/93	1993/94	Budget 1994/95
Profits and losses of public enterprises					
Number of operating enterprises (ND)	236	237	239	240	...
Profitable	125	135	133	123	...
Loss-making	111	102	106	117	...
Profit of profit-making public enterprisess (ND)[1]	53.9	60.8	73.8	97.2	...
Of which: In oil sector	23.0	18.0	23.3	39.5	...
Loss of loss-making public enterprises (ND)[1]	31.2	37.2	41.1	52.9	...
Losses of public enterprises (DP)	18.9	18.3	...	...	...
(In percent of GDP)	0.4	0.3	...	...	...
Losses of state electricity boards	41.7	48.9	47.0	...	...
(In percent of GDP)	0.8	0.8	0.6	...	...
Profit margins in selected sectors (ND)[1]					
Steel					
Public enterprises	−3.9	−5.8	−1.7	−1.1	...
Private	2.4	2.9	2.4	...	...
Fertilizer					
Public enterprises	−8.5	−7.5	−11.3	−8.0	...
Private	6.9	5.9	4.5	...	...
Chemicals and pharmaceuticals					
Public enterprises	−2.9	−3.1	1.5	−0.6	...
Private	4.3	4.7	5.0	...	...
Heavy engineering					
Public enterprises	−3.0	−2.7	−2.3	−7.9	...
Private	3.4	3.7	3.6	...	...
Textile					
Public enterprises	−16.7	−23.7	−39.2	−38.4	...
Private	3.9	2.3	2.2	...	...
Private gross profit over capital	22.2	21.7	19.8	19.8	...
All public enterprises' gross profit over capital	10.9	11.6	11.4	11.3	...
All public enterprises' net profit over capital	2.2	2.0	2.4	2.7	...
Financing of public enterprises' plan investments (ND and DP)					
Internal resources	107	120	161	189	229
Bonds and debentures[2]	49	57	63	62	75
External commercial[3]	26	19	37	41	72
Others (public deposit accounts)[4]	23	29	39	72	53
Budget support (ND)[5]	76	69	66	75	72
(In percent of GDP)	1.4	1.1	1.0	0.9	0.8
Total financing	281	294	366	439	501
(In percent of GDP)	5.3	4.8	5.2	5.5	5.6
Memorandum items:					
Total central plan	381	402	497	614	701
(In percent of GDP)	7.2	6.5	7.0	7.7	7.8

Sources: Ministry of Finance, *Economic Survey, 1994–95;* Ministry of Industry, *Public Enterprise Survey;* budget documents; Center for Monitoring of the Indian Economy; World Bank.

Note: DP = departmental (i.e., fall under government departments); ND = nondepartmental.

[1]Profits are net of taxes and relative to sales.

[2]Sold in domestic capital markets.

[3]Includes supplier's credit.

[4]Includes public deposit accounts and intercorporate borrowing.

[5]Includes loan and equity contributions, excludes subsidized grants.

tiles, fertilizer, steel, and heavy engineering).[33] Heavy capital investments in the past, combined with a large interest burden have reduced the profit margins of public enterprises. Annual net financing needs of public enterprises under the central government have exceeded 5 percent of GDP (about one fourth of domestic savings) in the last four years.

By all accounts, performance is much worse in the enterprises at the state level; in 1992/93 the losses of state electricity boards alone amounted to 14 percent of total plan outlays of states and union territories. Pricing policies are a major factor underlying the poor performance of these boards, as administered prices for electricity have often been fixed below the average cost of production excluding depreciation.[34]

The goals of public enterprise reform are greater efficiency, productivity, and competitiveness. The reforms have focused on (1) creating internal competition by eliminating entry barriers, subsidies, price distortions, and preferential access to budget and bank resources; (2) improving the management of public enterprises by increasing autonomy and the mandate to become profit-oriented centers; (3) introducing restructuring policies and establishing a social safety net program; and (4) implementing several rounds of divestment. Table 7.8 summarizes the progress to date in these areas and the medium-term objectives.

Competition Policies

Reforms in competition policies have been the most extensive. The number of areas reserved exclusively for the public sector has been reduced from 18 in 1991 to 6 (defense products, atomic energy, coal and lignite, mineral oils, railway transport, and radioactive minerals). Thus, public enterprises face competition in sectors as diverse as mining, oil refining, power, air transport, telecommunications, banking, and all lines of manufacturing. Trade liberalization and a more liberal foreign direct investment regime also added pressure for innovation and cost-effective production. Financial market reforms have created more equal and efficient financing opportunities, and fiscal reform has resulted in a harder budget constraint for most public enterprises.

However, as noted earlier, the expansion of private activity has at times been restricted by concerns regarding the ability of some public enterprises to compete effectively. Furthermore, reforms

at the state level are generally lagging behind, especially in the power sector, where the poor financial position of most state electricity boards limits their ability to pay for private power. Finally, there is scope for reducing subsidies by comprehensive price adjustments, especially for power, petroleum, and fertilizers.

Management Policies

Increasing competition for public enterprises has prompted changes in the organizational structure to provide more operational autonomy, including setting out in a memorandum of understanding (MoU) an objective basis for evaluating the management of a public enterprise by the ministry responsible for its administration. Although the MoU system now covers some 106 central public enterprises (about half of the total, including nearly all loss-makers), it does not appear to have achieved its objective of providing greater autonomy. In 1993/94, 75 percent of the evaluated public enterprises were rated "excellent" or "very good," and only 10 percent were rated "fair," suggesting that the criteria for ratings were not very stringent.

A key problem with the MoU system has been the lack of credible sanctions against management that fail to meet commitments in an MoU. Allowing effective restructuring of the public enterprise and implementing exit policies (including firing management) would be one route to strengthening sanctions. The MoU system could also be strengthened with more comprehensive multiyear contracts that further improve incentives, flexibility, and accountability. Another drawback is the conflict of interest inherent in an administrative ministry rating and supervising the public enterprises that fall under its jurisdiction.

Restructuring Policies

Since December 1991, 140 central and state enterprises have been referred to the BIFR, of which 56 cases meet the criteria of sickness. As discussed earlier, BIFR procedures have proven extremely cumbersome and none of the public enterprises recommended for closure has actually been shut down. In addition to strengthening BIFR procedures, overhauling labor policies, and improving the social safety net, there is also a need to identify loss-making public enterprises at an early stage rather than when they are already chronically sick.

Divestment Policies

Since October 1991, several rounds of divestment of shares in centrally owned public enterprises have raised some Rs 102 billion (equivalent to $3.6 billion

---

[33]The 1994–95 *Economic Survey* reports that out of the 15 large central public enterprises operating in the core sector, 7 are loss-makers (Ministry of Finance (1995)).

[34]Moreover, certain sectors such as agriculture receive highly preferential tariffs; in some states, electricity is provided free to farmers.

Table 7.8. Public Enterprise Reform: Progress to Date and Medium-Term Objectives

Status in 1991	Progress Through Mid-1995	Areas of Future Reform
Competition policies 1,000 public enterprises play a major role at central and state level.	Size of public enterprise sector has been contained.	Review portfolio of public sector investment, enhance competition, allow foreign investment.
18 industries reserved for public sector with variety of entry barriers and managed prices for power, petroleum, and fertilizer.	List of areas reserved for public sector gradually reduced.	Liberalization of insurance industry; further opening of air transport, railways, and oil; reform of power sector at state level.
Nearly 1.5 percent of GDP direct budgetary support to public enterprises in addition to a variety of subsidies, and financing at below market rates.	Budgetary support curtailed to 0.8 percent of GDP, financing in domestic capital markets increased, preferential access to bank credits eliminated.	Reduce indirect and state budgetary support; reduce subsidies for power, petroleum, and fertilizer.
Management policies Direct supervision of public enterprises from government.	Managerial autonomy marginally improved through memorandum of understanding (MoU) (104 signed in 1993/94).	Create profit centers, improve accountability, create multiyear MoU, improve incentives.
Risk-averse management, public enterprise returns often below market cost of capital (net profits below 2 percent of capital), low export earnings.	Marginal improvement in profitability (2.4 percent net profits over capital), improved export earnings, retraining of managers.	Expand flexibility of MoU system to enhance competition, allow restructuring at firm level, and modify exit policies.
	Minority share in 34 public enterprises divested (limited to 49 percent), mainly in manufacturing sector; technical problems and political resistance to further divestment.	Diversify privatization across sectors; raise limits on private ownership in selected industries.
Restructuring policies Public sector has some 54 chronically sick firms employing more than 300,000 workers.	140 public enterprises referred to BIFR, but none closed; law to liquidate public enterprises adopted in December 1991.	Enforce sick industrial companies act (1993) to implement remedial measures in sick public enterprises, reduce exemptions in bankruptcy law.
Lack of social safety net for unemployment.	Establishment of National Renewal Fund (NRF) in 1991, which financed retirement of 60,000 workers in 40 public enterprises.	Strengthen NRF by improved targeting of funds.

or about 1.4 percent of average annual GDP for the period). So far, divestment has been limited to a maximum of 49 percent of equity and has covered 35 profitable central public enterprises concentrated mainly in the manufacturing sector.[35] On average, some 15 percent of the shares in these companies have been sold, with the highest being 43 percent in the case of Hindustan Organic Chemicals (Table 7.9). Central government holdings have been reduced to less than 60 percent in only three of these companies.

The divestment program has had mixed success, in part because the objective of raising revenue has often superseded the objective of improving efficiency. Initially, bids were invited for a basket of company shares; later bidding for individual shares was allowed. The investor base was gradually widened to include a full range of domestic investors and foreign institutional investors. The government expects to raise an additional Rs 70 billion from divestment in 1995/96, possibly by allowing sales through fixed-price offers rather than auctions, which would allow tapping of a broader investor base.

Unless they serve a clear social purpose, most public enterprises should eventually be privatized. As a transitional step, it would be important to accelerate the divestment program, extending the process to a broader range of companies and also reducing government share holdings below 51 percent in at

---

[35]Divestment programs for public enterprises owned by states have been more ambitious as some enterprises have been sold outright.

Table 7.9. Public Sector Enterprises: Divestment
(In percent)

Name of Company	Equity Divested					Government Share
	1991/92	1992/93	1993/94	1994/95	Total	
1. Andrew Yule	13.6	—	—	—	13.6	55.0
2. Bharat Earthmovers Ltd.	20.0	—	5.0	—	25.0	62.0
3. Bharat Electronics Ltd.	20.0	—	4.0	—	24.0	64.0
4. Bharat Heavy Electricals Ltd.	20.0	—	11.0	—	31.0	58.0
5. Bharat Petroleum Corporation Ltd.	20.0	10.0	—	—	30.0	62.0
6. Bongaigaon Refinery & Petrochemicals Ltd.	20.0	5.0	—	—	25.0	69.6
7. CMC Ltd.	16.7	—	—	—	16.7	83.3
8. Cochin Refineries Ltd.	10.0	—	—	—	10.0	55.0
9. Container Corporation of India	—	—	—	20.0	20.0	80.0
10. Dredging Corporation of India Ltd.	1.4	—	—	—	1.4	98.0
11. Fertilizers & Chemicals (Travancore) Ltd.	1.5	0.2	—	—	1.7	97.3
12. Hindustan Cables Ltd.	3.6	—	—	—	3.6	96.4
13. Hindustan Machine Tools Ltd.	5.4	5.0	—	—	10.4	86.0
14. Hindustan Organic Chemicals Ltd.	20.0	—	—	23.1	43.1	56.9
15. Hindustan Petroleum Corporation Ltd.	20.0	10.0	7.0	—	37.0	62.7
16. Hindustan Photofilms Manufacturing Company Ltd.	16.1	—	—	—	16.1	83.9
17. Hindustan Zinc Ltd.	20.0	5.1	—	—	25.1	74.9
18. Indian Oil Corporation	—	—	—	10.0	10.0	88.1
19. Indian Petrochemicals Corporation Ltd.	20.0	—	—	—	20.0	62.4
20. Indian Railway Construction Co. Ltd.	0.3	—	—	—	0.3	99.0
21. Indian Telephone Industries	20.0	1.1	—	—	21.1	65.0
22. Madras Refineries Ltd.	16.9	—	15.9	—	32.8	51.8
23. Mahanagar Telephone Nigam Ltd.	20.0	—	13.0	—	33.0	60.0
24. Maruti Udyog Ltd.	9.0	—	—	—	9.0	90.3
25. Minerals & Metals Trading Corporation	0.7	—	—	—	0.7	97.0
26. National Aluminium Company Ltd.	2.7	10.0	—	—	12.7	87.2
27. National Fertilizers Ltd.	2.3	0.1	—	...	2.4	97.6
28. Neyveli Lignite Corporation	5.0	2.2	—	—	7.2	92.8
29. Oil and Natural Gas Corporation	—	—	—	2.0	2.0	98.0
30. Rashtriya Chemicals & Fertilizers Ltd.	5.6	1.9	—	—	7.5	92.5
31. Shipping Corporation of India	20.0	—	—	1.4	21.4	67.6
32. State Trading Corporation	8.0	0.1	—	—	8.1	90.0
33. Steel Authority of India Ltd.	5.0	5.5	—	0.1	10.6	88.9
34. Videsh Sanchar Nigam Ltd.	15.0	—	—	—	15.0	85.0

Source: Ministry of Finance (1995).

least a few key enterprises. The report of the Rangarajan Committee on Divestment of Shares in Public Sector Enterprises proposed majority or full privatization of selected enterprises in sectors where there is no compelling rationale for public participation (Rangarajan and others (1993)). This report—completed in March 1993—has not yet been adopted by the government.

Financial Market Reform

Prior to the latest round of reforms, the financial system in India was severely repressed. As in other such regimes, the government intervened in the market for a variety of reasons—to finance the fiscal deficit at low cost, to subsidize strategic industries, to provide support for the underprivileged, and to control markets directly in the absence of indirect instruments of monetary control.

The government pre-empted a substantial portion of available financial savings through the cash reserve requirement (CRR) and the statutory liquidity ratio (SLR) imposed on bank deposits. Moreover, administered lending and deposit rates created distortions in both savings and the demand for credit. Directed credit programs further contributed to resource misallocation and weakened the credit analysis function of banks. In a context of inadequate prudential regulations and bank supervision, these distortions resulted in the accumulation of nonperforming assets. The lack of competition implied by a predominantly government-owned banking system also contributed to costly yet poor quality financial services.[36]

Wide-ranging reform measures implemented since 1991 have sought to make the financial system more market oriented, thereby increasing its efficiency. In the banking sector, these reforms have included interest rate deregulation, a phased reduction of the cash reserve requirement and the statutory liquidity ratio, simplifying directed credit programs, development of money markets, relaxation of barriers to entry for private banks, and measures to strengthen banks' balance sheets, including through capital replenishments and tighter prudential regulations and supervision (see Table 7.10 for details). Similarly, capital market reforms have aimed at improving market efficiency, making transactions more transparent, curbing unfair trade practices, and establishing an effective regulatory framework.

Progress in Reducing Interest Rate Distortions

Prior to 1991, a multitude of fixed lending and deposit rates favored borrowers in small-scale industry and agriculture (the "priority sectors") and offered relatively low yields on longer-term savings. The rates were adjusted periodically in light of changing macroeconomic circumstances; however, this sometimes occurred with a lag, resulting in negative real interest rates. This complex structure of administered rates was simplified in 1992/93. A small number of fixed rates for priority sector loans were retained, while larger commercial borrowers faced a floor lending rate. Bank deposit rates were subject only to a single ceiling rate. This system guaranteed banks a minimum interest rate spread and a measure of protection against mounting losses.

In 1993/94, the markets for commercial paper and certificates of deposit were deregulated, allowing companies to access credit at market terms that were considerably below the minimum lending rate. In October 1994, the minimum lending rate was eliminated. At present, the remaining interest rate controls comprise two fixed rates (12 percent and 13.5 percent) for small- and medium-sized borrowers and the maximum deposit rate (12 percent). The deregulation of interest rates has been accompanied by a variety of other measures that have given banks greater flexibility in setting credit limits, screening borrowers, and participating in consortium arrangements.

Prior to the deregulation of lending rates, the gap between the minimum lending rate and the equilibrium market rate (proxied by the discount rate on commercial bills) had narrowed from 4.7 percentage points in 1989/90 to an average of 3.2 percentage points in 1992/93–1993/94 (Table 7.11). Although the "Montiel measure" of the lending rate gap fell from 41.6 percent in 1989/90 to an average of 27 percent in 1991/92–1993/94, it remained fairly high.[37] The gap between the maximum deposit rate and the market rate (proxied by the interest rates on certificates of deposit) also decreased from 3.9 percentage points in 1990/91 to an average of 2.8 percentage points in 1993/94–1994/95. However, the Montiel measure (22.6 percent in 1994/95) is not much below than that prior to 1991, suggesting that the repression of deposit rates has not been significantly reduced.

The spread between lending and deposit rates fell from 5 percentage points in 1990/91 to 3 percentage points in early 1995/96.[38] The wedge created by nonremuneration of the cash reserve requirement contributed about 2 percentage points to the spread in 1994/95.[39] Subsidies implicit in priority sector credits, loan losses, and high operating costs (owing to considerable overstaffing in the banking system) also contributed to the spread.

Growth and Development of Financial Markets

As measured by the ratio of various monetary aggregates to GDP, there has been some financial deepening since 1991. The ratio of broad money (M3) to GDP rose from about 50 percent in 1990/91 to 56 percent in 1994/95 (Table 7.12). The rapid growth of time and savings deposits largely accounted for the increase; narrow money (currency and demand deposits) increased by about 2 percentage points of GDP during this period.

Nevertheless, there is evidence of disintermediation from the banking system since the late 1980s, both because of the disincentives created by interest rate controls and the emergence of alternative financial instruments. The share of bank deposits in

---

[36]For a discussion of the problems of the banking sector and reform of the financial system see, for example, Ministry of Finance (1993), Khatkhate (1993), Iyer (1994), Nayak (1993), and Rangarajan (1994). The Reserve Bank of India's Annual Reports and Reports on Currency and Finance also contain details regarding the financial sector.

[37]The Montiel measure is the ratio of the gap between market and regulated rates to the market rate. That is, $[(i_m - i_r)/i_m] \times 100$, where i_m is the market interest rate, and i_r is the regulated interest rate.

[38]The spread refers to the difference between the maximum deposit rate (12 percent) and the newly deregulated prime rate. The corresponding percentage spread (that is, the ratio of the spread between lending and deposit rates to the deposit rate) fell from 45 percent to 27 percent.

[39]To compute the impact of the cash reserve requirement on the interest rate spread, it is assumed that banks have no operating costs, no defaults, and are perfectly competitive. Then, $i_1/i_d = 1/(1 - r)$, where i_1 and i_d are the nominal loan and deposit rates and r is the reserve requirement.

Table 7.10. Financial Sector Reform: Progress to Date and Future Reform Areas

Status Before July 1991	Status in Mid-1995	Areas of Future Reform
Interest rate controls Bank lending rates fixed according to loan size and sector specific categories (loans over Rs 200,000 had an interest rate floor).	Interest rate structure simplified. Interest rate floor on loans over Rs 200,000 eliminated.	Eliminate remaining controls.
Bank deposit rates fixed according to account types and maturities.	Fixed interest rates on term deposits replaced by an interest rate ceiling.	Liberalize the deposit rates to permit market-determined rates.
Interest rates on certificates of deposit (CDs) are free but there is a bankwise limit on issuance.	Bankwise limit on issuance of CDs abolished.	
Government pre-emptions Government pre-empted large proportion of bank reserves through cash reserve ratio (CRR) and statutory liquidity ratio (SLR): CRR of 25 percent and SLR of 38.5 percent of deposits.	Government pre-emptions reduced. CRR lowered to 15 percent and effective SLR to 29.3 percent (25 percent at the margin).	Phase out SLR and reduce CRR to about 10 percent.
High monetization of government debt.	Monetization has been reduced.	Phase out monetization with further fiscal consolidation and development of the government bond market.
Directed credit At least 40 percent of bank credit channeled to the priority sectors at concessional interest rate.	Number of directed credit categories and interest rate subsidy element reduced.	Reduction in the size of the directed credit.
Prudential regulations and financial supervision Inadequate norms concerning income recognition, provisioning, and capital adequacy severely weakened financial condition of banks.	Regulations on asset classification, income recognition, provisioning, and capital adequacy strengthened. Recapitalization of banks actively pursued along with rationalization of their management. Board for Financial Supervision set up to strengthen the supervision of banks and nonbank financial intermediaries.	Prudential regulation and financial supervision should be further strengthened, especially those governing risk exposure, conflict of interest, moral hazard, transparency, and concentration of loans.
Capital market Issuing as well as pricing of the securities strictly controlled by Controller of Capital Issues, thus hampering development and efficiency of securities market.	Firms are free to issue and price securities. Controller of Capital Issues abolished. Securities Exchange Board of India set up to protect investors and enhance transparency of the capital market. Indian firms in good standing allowed to issue securities abroad. Foreign institutional investors allowed to invest in the domestic capital market. National Stock Exchange of India began operation on a screen-based trading system. Private sector mutual funds were set up. Over the counter market was set up.	Further measures to liberalize, open, and deepen the capital market. In particular, improve payment, settlement, and clearing system, as well as legal and regulatory infrastructure.
Controls on interest rates on government securities.	Government securities are auctioned. Primary dealer system for government securities introduced.	
Competition policy Highly concentrated market with strict entry as well as branching rules.	Guideline for entry of new private banks formulated, and new private banks set up. Restrictions on opening of new bank branches as well as closing of unviable ones relaxed. Government share of equity in public banks brought down. Equity participation in new banks by foreign institutional investors.	Further relaxation of entry and exit barriers. Abolish remaining government interventions on asset, liability, and labor management. Further opening of the financial market to foreign competition.
Government monopoly of the insurance market.	No change.	Open insurance to private sector competition.

Sources: Indian authorities; and IMF staff.

Table 7.11. Effects of the Reform on Interest Rate Structure

(End of period; in percent unless otherwise noted)

	1987/88	1988/89	1989/90	1990/91	1991/92	1992/93	1993/94	1994/95
Lending rates								
Regulated rate[1]	16.5	16.0	16.0	16.0	19.0	17.0	14.0	15.0
Market rate[2]	. . .	12.8	11.3	12.0	15.0	14.5	10.2	15.0
Market rate – regulated rate	. . .	–3.2	–4.7	–4.0	–4.0	–2.5	–3.8	—
Montiel measure[3]	. . .	–25.0	–41.6	–33.3	–26.7	–17.2	–37.3	—
Real regulated rate	5.8	10.3	6.9	3.9	5.4	10.0	3.2	5.0
Real market rate	. . .	7.1	2.2	–0.1	1.4	7.5	–0.6	5.0
Deposit rates								
Regulated rate[4]	10.0	10.0	10.0	11.0	13.0	11.0	10.0	12.0[5]
Market rate[6]	. . .	14.0	13.5	14.9	17.0	16.5	12.0	15.5
Market rate – regulated rate	. . .	4.0	3.5	3.9	4.0	5.5	2.0	3.5
Montiel measure[3]	. . .	28.6	25.9	26.2	23.5	33.3	16.7	22.6
Real regulated rate	–0.7	4.3	0.9	–1.1	–0.6	4.0	–0.8	2.0
Real market rate	. . .	8.3	4.4	2.8	3.4	9.5	1.2	5.5
Interest margin								
Lending rate – deposit rate (regulated)[1,4]	6.5	6.0	6.0	5.0	6.0	6.0	4.0	3.0

Sources: Reserve Bank of India, *Annual Report*, various issues, and *Report on Currency and Finance*, various issues; and IMF staff estimates.

[1]Commercial bank minimum lending rate. For 1994/95, liberalized bank lending rate (prime rate).
[2]Lower limit of discount rates on commercial bills.
[3]{(Market interest rate – regulated interest rate)/market interest rate} × 100.
[4]From 1992/93, commercial bank deposit rate ceiling. Before 1992/93, highest fixed deposit rate.
[5]Deposit rate ceiling as of April 1995.
[6]Upper limit of interest rates on certificates of deposit.

Table 7.12. Effects of the Reform on Financial Market Structure

	1987/88	1988/89	1989/90	1990/91	1991/92	1992/93	1993/94	1994/95
				(In percent of GDP)				
Financial deepening								
Broad money (end of period)	48.8	48.5	50.4	49.6	51.5	52.2	55.1	56.0
				(In percent of total)				
Households' savings in financial assets								
Bank deposits	40.6	36.9	30.1	29.2	29.3	35.3	37.3	. . .
Nonbank financial assets	59.4	63.1	69.9	70.8	70.7	64.7	62.7	. . .
Shares and debentures	2.3	2.8	5.5	8.7	9.3	10.0	8.8	. . .
Commercial financing								
Domestic financing	99.4	99.2	97.4	96.3	97.9	99.9	84.9	. . .
Bank loans	66.3	68.0	61.9	53.0	34.4	46.7	37.0	. . .
Nonbank loans	15.0	14.3	19.1	25.6	35.7	27.4	11.4	. . .
Shares and debentures	18.1	16.9	16.4	17.7	27.8	25.8	36.4	. . .
Foreign financing	0.5	0.7	2.5	3.6	2.2	0.2	15.1	. . .
Memorandum items:								
Government pre-emption at margin (CRR + SLR) (in percent)	58.0	59.0	53.0	53.5	63.5	45.0	39.0	40.0
Priority sector credit (in percent of gross bank credit; end of period)	41.4	39.9	39.3	36.4	36.1	33.9	34.4	. . .
Money multiplier	3.05	3.07	2.98	3.03	3.19	3.31	3.13	3.12

Sources: Reserve Bank of India, *Annual Report*, various issues, and *Report on Currency and Finance*, various issues; and IMF staff estimates.

households' financial savings declined from 41 percent in 1987/88 to 29 percent in 1990/91, partly owing to the impact of inflation on real returns. As prices began to stabilize, bank deposits recovered to 37 percent of household savings in 1993/94. By contrast, savings held as equity and debentures showed strong growth during this period; their combined share rose from about 2 percent in 1987/88 to 9 percent in 1993/94.

On the lending side, the pattern is similar. The share of bank borrowing in total commercial financing declined from 68 percent in the late 1980s to 37 percent in 1993/94. Financing from capital markets increased from 16 percent to 36 percent over the same period, while the share of foreign financing rose from 3 percent to 15 percent. The liberalization of capital markets, particularly the ability of firms to raise capital without prior approval, has led to a rapid expansion of both public stock issues and rights issues.[40]

The proportion of bank deposits pre-empted by the government through the mechanism of cash reserve requirements or statutory liquidity ratios has gradually been reduced. The combined marginal rate declined from 54 percent in 1990/91 to 40 percent in 1994/95. The development of a primary market in government securities has facilitated the reduction in the cash reserve requirement and statutory liquidity ratio; a large proportion of the public sector's borrowing requirement is now met through market borrowing. The pace of reduction of the cash reserve requirement and statutory liquidity ratio, however, has been constrained by the continued large financing needs of the public sector.

Forty percent of bank credit must still be directed to priority sectors, although the subsidy element has been reduced and the definition of priority industries (some of which are not subsidized) has been expanded to make it easier for banks to comply with the guidelines.[41]

---

[40]The 1,032 issues launched during April–December 1994 were 37 percent higher than issues in the same period a year earlier.

[41]The 1995/96 budget requires that banks not meeting the agricultural lending guidelines deposit a part of the shortfall with the National Bank for Agriculture and Rural Development. The resources will be directed toward rural infrastructure programs.

Future Priorities

Considerable progress has been made over the last several years in restructuring the domestic banking system. However, additional reforms are still needed to ensure that this important sector provides a sound foundation for growth in the rest of the economy.

At 15 percent, the cash reserve requirement remains at its 1990/91 level—well above the authorities' target of 10 percent for 1996/97, and a substantial tax on intermediation through the banking system. Even if the cash reserve requirement and statutory liquidity ratio were lowered to their target levels by 1996/97, some 35 percent of bank deposits would still be channeled to the public sector. Continued reliance on the statutory liquidity ratio sends a signal that the government must still rely on financial controls to manage its fiscal affairs.

It will also be important to develop longer-term money markets as well as an active secondary market in government securities. Such steps would permit greater reliance on indirect instruments of monetary control. Additional measures to strengthen the commercial banks are also essential. In the face of increased competition from new private banks and capital markets, government-owned banks will need to reduce their costs further and find a definitive solution to the problem of nonperforming assets. Stronger prudential regulations and supervision are crucial and would allow complete deregulation of bank deposit rates as moral hazard is reduced. Improved management systems and greater operational autonomy for government-owned banks are also needed. Finally, the government has not accepted the Narasimham Committee's recommendation to reduce the share of priority credit in bank loans and advances to 10 percent and, as noted, two fifths of bank credit must still be directed to priority sectors (Narasimham (1991)).

In the equities market, risks of disruption remain that could retard market development or trigger an outflow of portfolio capital. The proposed central depository system should help to improve market transparency and efficiency, while the primary dealer system will add depth and liquidity to the government securities market. The establishment of a regulatory body for the insurance industry will be an important step toward private participation in that sector.

VIII References

Ahluwalia, Isher Judge, *Productivity and Growth in Indian Manufacturing* (New Delhi: Oxford University Press, 1991).

———— "The Manufacturing Sector in India," in *India: Industrial Development Review* (London: Economist Intelligence Unit, and Vienna: United Nations Industrial Development Organization, 1995).

Anant, T.C.A., Tamal Datta Chaudhuri, Shubhashis Gangopadhyay, and Omkar Goswami, "Industrial Sickness in India: Institutional Responses and Issues in Restructuring" (unpublished; New Delhi, April 1994).

Aziz, Jahangir, "Discretionary Trading and Asset Price Volatility," IMF Working Paper No. 95/104 (Washington: International Monetary Fund, October 1995).

Balakrishnan P., and K. Pushpangadan, "Total Factor-Productivity Growth in Manufacturing Industry: A Fresh Look," *Economic and Political Weekly,* July 30, 1994, pp. 2028–35.

Barro, Robert J., and Jong-Wha Lee, "International Comparisons of Educational Attainment," *Journal of Monetary Economics,* Vol. 32 (December 1993), pp. 363–94.

Bhattacharya, B., *Policy Impediments to Foreign Direct Investment in India: Status and Issues* (New Delhi: Indian Institute of Foreign Trade, 1994).

Cashin, Paul, and Ratna Sahay, "Internal Migration, Center-State Grants and Economic Growth in the States of India," IMF Working Paper No. 95/66 (Washington: International Monetary Fund, July 1995).

Confederation of Indian Industry, "The States: Strategy for Growth," background paper on administrative reforms prepared for the 20th annual session (Calcutta, 1994).

Dixit, Avinash K., and Robert S. Pindyck, *Investment Under Uncertainty* (Princeton, New Jersey: Princeton University Press, 1994).

Dunaway, Steven, and others, *Private Market Financing for Developing Countries*, World Economic and Financial Surveys (Washington: International Monetary Fund, 1995).

Fischer, Stanley, "The Role of Macroeconomic Factors in Growth," *Journal of Monetary Economics,* Vol. 32 (December 1993), pp. 485–512.

Goldsbrough, David, and others, *The Response of Investment and Growth to Adjustment Policies: Lessons from Eight Countries* (Washington: International Monetary Fund, forthcoming).

Goldstein, Morris, and David Folkerts-Landau, *International Capital Markets: Developments, Prospects, and Policy Issues,* World Economic and Financial Surveys (Washington: International Monetary Fund, 1994).

Goswami, Omkar, and others, *Report of the Committee on Industrial Sickness and Corporate Restructuring* (New Delhi, 1993).

Greene, Joshua, and Delano Villanueva, "Private Investment in Developing Countries: An Empirical Analysis," *Staff Papers*, International Monetary Fund, Vol. 38 (March 1991), pp. 33–58.

Hodrick, Robert, and Edward C. Prescott, "Postwar U.S. Business Cycles: An Empirical Investigation" (unpublished; Carnegie-Mellon University 1980).

Industrial Credit and Investment Corporation of India Limited, *Capacity Utilization in the Private Corporate Sector, 1991–92 and 1992–93* (Bombay, 1994).

International Finance Corporation (1994a), *Emerging Stock Markets: Factbook* (Washington, 1994).

———— (1994b), *Quarterly Review of Emerging Markets,* First Quarter (Washington, 1994).

International Labor Organization, *India: Employment, Poverty and Economic Policies* (New Delhi, December 1993).

International Monetary Fund, *World Economic Outlook, October 1994: A Survey by the Staff of the International Monetary Fund,* World Economic and Financial Surveys (Washington, 1994).

Iyer, T.N. Anantharam, "The Evolution of the Money Market and Government Securities Market in India," background paper for the Sixth Seminar on Central Banking, International Monetary Fund (Washington, 1994).

Joshi, Vijay, and I.M.D. Little, *India: Macroeconomics and Political Economy 1964–91* (Washington: World Bank, 1994).

Khatkhate, Deena, "Indian Banking System: Restitution and Reform Sequencing" (unpublished; Washington, 1993).

King, Robert G., and Ross Levine, "Capital Fundamentalism, Economic Development and Economic Growth," *Carnegie-Rochester Series on Public Policy,* Vol. 40 (June 1994), pp. 259–92.

Kirmani, Naheed, and others, *International Trade Policies: The Uruguay Round and Beyond,* World Economic and Financial Surveys (Washington: International Monetary Fund, 1994).

Mankiw, N. Gregory, David Romer, and David N. Weil, "A Contribution to the Empirics of Economic Growth," *Quarterly Journal of Economics,* Vol. 107 (May 1992), pp. 407–38.

McCarthy, F. Desmond, J. Peter Neary, and Giovanni Zanalda, "Measuring the Effect of External Shocks and the Policy Response to Them: Empirical Methodology Applied to the Philippines," Policy Research Working Paper WPS 1271 (Washington: World Bank, March 1994).

Ministry of Finance, "Public Sector Commercial Banks and Financial Sector Reform: Rebuilding for a Better Future," Discussion Paper (New Delhi, 1993).

————, *Report of the Tenth Finance Commission (for 1995–2000)* (New Delhi, 1994).

————, *Economic Survey, 1994–95* (New Delhi, 1995).

Ministry of Industry, Department of Public Enterprises, *Public Enterprises Survey, 1993–94* (New Delhi, 1995).

Mohan, Rakesh, "Public Sector Reform and Issues in Privatization," paper presented at a meeting organized by the OECD Development Center and Center for Policy Research, New Delhi, March 6–7, 1995.

Narasimham, M., *Report of the Committee on the Financial System* (New Delhi, 1991).

Nayak, P. Jayendra, "The Reform of India's Financial System" (unpublished; New Delhi, 1993).

Pradhan, B.K., D.K. Ratha, and Atul Sarma, "Complementarity Between Public and Private Investment in India," *Journal of Development Economics,* Vol. 33 (July 1990), pp. 101–16.

Pursell, Garry, and Ashok Gulati, "Liberalizing Indian Agriculture: An Agenda for Reform," Policy Research Working Paper WPS 1172 (Washington: World Bank, September 1993).

Psacharopoulos, George, "Returns to Investment in Education: A Global Update," Policy Research Working Paper WPS 1067 (Washington: World Bank, January 1993).

Rama, Martin, "Empirical Investment Equations for Developing Countries," in *Striving for Growth After Adjustment: The Role of Capital Formation,* ed. by Luis Servén and Andrés Solimano (Washington: World Bank, 1993).

Rangarajan, C., and others, *Report of the Committee on Divestment of Shares in Public Sector Enterprises* (New Delhi, 1993).

————, "Developing the Money and Securities Markets in India," paper presented at the Sixth Seminar on Central Banking, International Monetary Fund (Washington, 1994).

Reserve Bank of India, *Annual Report, 1993–94* (Bombay, 1994).

————, *Report on Currency and Finance, 1994–95* (Bombay, 1995).

Summers, Robert, and Alan Heston, "The Penn World Table (Mark 5): An Expanded Set of International Comparisons, 1950–88," *Quarterly Journal of Economics,* Vol. 106 (May 1991), pp. 327–68.

————, The Penn World Table (Mark 5.6) database (1994).

Sundararajan, V., and Subhash Thakur, "Public Investment, Crowding Out, and Growth: A Dynamic Model Applied to India and Korea," *Staff Papers,* International Monetary Fund, Vol. 27 (December 1980), pp. 814–55.

Tax Reforms Committee (chaired by Raja J. Chelliah), *Final Report,* Parts I and II (New Delhi: Ministry of Finance, 1993).

World Bank, "India: Issues in Trade Reform," Report No. 13169-IN (Washington, 1994).

————, "India: Country Economic Memorandum, Recent Economic Developments: Achievements and Challenges," Report No. 14402-IN (Washington, 1995).

Recent Occasional Papers of the International Monetary Fund

134. India: Economic Reform and Growth, by Ajai Chopra, Charles Collyns, Richard Hemming, and Karen Parker with Woosik Chu and Oliver Fratzscher. 1995.

133. Policy Experiences and Issues in the Baltics, Russia, and Other Countries of the Former Soviet Union, edited by Daniel A. Citrin and Ashok K. Lahiri. 1995.

132. Financial Fragilities in Latin America: The 1980s and 1990s, by Liliana Rojas-Suárez and Steven R. Weisbrod. 1995.

131. Capital Account Convertibility: Review of Experience and Implications for IMF Policies, by staff teams headed by Peter J. Quirk and Owen Evans. 1995.

130. Challenges to the Swedish Welfare State, by Desmond Lachman, Adam Bennett, John H. Green, Robert Hagemann, and Ramana Ramaswamy. 1995.

129. IMF Conditionality: Experience Under Stand-By and Extended Arrangements. Part II: Background Papers. Susan Schadler, Editor, with Adam Bennett, Maria Carkovic, Louis Dicks-Mireaux, Mauro Mecagni, James H.J. Morsink, and Miguel A. Savastano. 1995.

128. IMF Conditionality: Experience Under Stand-By and Extended Arrangements. Part I: Key Issues and Findings, by Susan Schadler, Adam Bennett, Maria Carkovic, Louis Dicks-Mireaux, Mauro Mecagni, James H.J. Morsink, and Miguel A. Savastano. 1995.

127. Road Maps of the Transition: The Baltics, the Czech Republic, Hungary, and Russia, by Biswajit Banerjee, Vincent Koen, Thomas Krueger, Mark S. Lutz, Michael Marrese, and Tapio O. Saavalainen. 1995.

126. The Adoption of Indirect Instruments of Monetary Policy, by a Staff Team headed by William E. Alexander, Tomás J.T. Baliño, and Charles Enoch and comprising Francesco Caramazza, George Iden, David Marston, Johannes Mueller, Ceyla Pazarbasioglu, Marc Quintyn, Matthew Saal, and Gabriel Sensenbrenner. 1995.

125. United Germany: The First Five Years—Performance and Policy Issues, by Robert Corker, Robert A. Feldman, Karl Habermeier, Hari Vittas, and Tessa van der Willigen. 1995.

124. Saving Behavior and the Asset Price "Bubble" in Japan: Analytical Studies, edited by Ulrich Baumgartner and Guy Meredith. 1995.

123. Comprehensive Tax Reform: The Colombian Experience, edited by Parthasarathi Shome. 1995.

122. Capital Flows in the APEC Region, edited by Mohsin S. Khan and Carmen M. Reinhart. 1995.

121. Uganda: Adjustment with Growth, 1987–94, by Robert L. Sharer, Hema R. De Zoysa, and Calvin A. McDonald. 1995.

120. Economic Dislocation and Recovery in Lebanon, by Sena Eken, Paul Cashin, S. Nuri Erbas, Jose Martelino, and Adnan Mazarei. 1995.

119. Singapore: A Case Study in Rapid Development, edited by Kenneth Bercuson with a staff team comprising Robert G. Carling, Aasim M. Husain, Thomas Rumbaugh, and Rachel van Elkan. 1995.

118. Sub-Saharan Africa: Growth, Savings, and Investment, by Michael T. Hadjimichael, Dhaneshwar Ghura, Martin Mühleisen, Roger Nord, and E. Murat Uçer. 1995.

117. Resilience and Growth Through Sustained Adjustment: The Moroccan Experience, by Saleh M. Nsouli, Sena Eken, Klaus Enders, Van-Can Thai, Jörg Decressin, and Filippo Cartiglia, with Janet Bungay. 1995.

116. Improving the International Monetary System: Constraints and Possibilities, by Michael Mussa, Morris Goldstein, Peter B. Clark, Donald J. Mathieson, and Tamim Bayoumi. 1994.

115. Exchange Rates and Economic Fundamentals: A Framework for Analysis, by Peter B. Clark, Leonardo Bartolini, Tamim Bayoumi, and Steven Symansky. 1994.

114. Economic Reform in China: A New Phase, by Wanda Tseng, Hoe Ee Khor, Kalpana Kochhar, Dubravko Mihaljek, and David Burton. 1994.

113. Poland: The Path to a Market Economy, by Liam P. Ebrill, Ajai Chopra, Charalambos Christofides, Paul Mylonas, Inci Otker, and Gerd Schwartz. 1994.

112. The Behavior of Non-Oil Commodity Prices, by Eduardo Borensztein, Mohsin S. Khan, Carmen M. Reinhart, and Peter Wickham. 1994.

111. The Russian Federation in Transition: External Developments, by Benedicte Vibe Christensen. 1994.

110. Limiting Central Bank Credit to the Government: Theory and Practice, by Carlo Cottarelli. 1993.

109. The Path to Convertibility and Growth: The Tunisian Experience, by Saleh M. Nsouli, Sena Eken, Paul Duran, Gerwin Bell, and Zühtü Yücelik. 1993.

108. Recent Experiences with Surges in Capital Inflows, by Susan Schadler, Maria Carkovic, Adam Bennett, and Robert Kahn. 1993.

107. China at the Threshold of a Market Economy, by Michael W. Bell, Hoe Ee Khor, and Kalpana Kochhar with Jun Ma, Simon N'guiamba, and Rajiv Lall. 1993.

106. Economic Adjustment in Low-Income Countries: Experience Under the Enhanced Structural Adjustment Facility, by Susan Schadler, Franek Rozwadowski, Siddharth Tiwari, and David O. Robinson. 1993.

105. The Structure and Operation of the World Gold Market, by Gary O'Callaghan. 1993.

104. Price Liberalization in Russia: Behavior of Prices, Household Incomes, and Consumption During the First Year, by Vincent Koen and Steven Phillips. 1993.

103. Liberalization of the Capital Account: Experiences and Issues, by Donald J. Mathieson and Liliana Rojas-Suárez. 1993.

102. Financial Sector Reforms and Exchange Arrangements in Eastern Europe. Part I: Financial Markets and Intermediation, by Guillermo A. Calvo and Manmohan S. Kumar. Part II: Exchange Arrangements of Previously Centrally Planned Economies, by Eduardo Borensztein and Paul R. Masson. 1993.

101. Spain: Converging with the European Community, by Michel Galy, Gonzalo Pastor, and Thierry Pujol. 1993.

100. The Gambia: Economic Adjustment in a Small Open Economy, by Michael T. Hadjimichael, Thomas Rumbaugh, and Eric Verreydt. 1992.

99. Mexico: The Strategy to Achieve Sustained Economic Growth, edited by Claudio Loser and Eliot Kalter. 1992.

98. Albania: From Isolation Toward Reform, by Mario I. Blejer, Mauro Mecagni, Ratna Sahay, Richard Hides, Barry Johnston, Piroska Nagy, and Roy Pepper. 1992.

97. Rules and Discretion in International Economic Policy, by Manuel Guitián. 1992.

96. Policy Issues in the Evolving International Monetary System, by Morris Goldstein, Peter Isard, Paul R. Masson, and Mark P. Taylor. 1992.

95. The Fiscal Dimensions of Adjustment in Low-Income Countries, by Karim Nashashibi, Sanjeev Gupta, Claire Liuksila, Henri Lorie, and Walter Mahler. 1992.

94. Tax Harmonization in the European Community: Policy Issues and Analysis, edited by George Kopits. 1992.

93. Regional Trade Arrangements, by Augusto de la Torre and Margaret R. Kelly. 1992.

92. Stabilization and Structural Reform in the Czech and Slovak Federal Republic: First Stage, by Bijan B. Aghevli, Eduardo Borensztein, and Tessa van der Willigen. 1992.

91. Economic Policies for a New South Africa, edited by Desmond Lachman and Kenneth Bercuson with a staff team comprising Daudi Ballali, Robert Corker, Charalambos Christofides, and James Wein. 1992.

90. The Internationalization of Currencies: An Appraisal of the Japanese Yen, by George S. Tavlas and Yuzuru Ozeki. 1992.

89. The Romanian Economic Reform Program, by Dimitri G. Demekas and Mohsin S. Khan. 1991.

88. Value-Added Tax: Administrative and Policy Issues, edited by Alan A. Tait. 1991.

87. Financial Assistance from Arab Countries and Arab Regional Institutions, by Pierre van den Boogaerde. 1991.

86. Ghana: Adjustment and Growth, 1983–91, by Ishan Kapur, Michael T. Hadjimichael, Paul Hilbers, Jerald Schiff, and Philippe Szymczak. 1991.

Note: For information on the title and availability of Occasional Papers not listed, please consult the IMF Publications Catalog or contact IMF Publication Services.